THE NEW UNBLOCKED ~~College~~ ~~ng Centre~~ MANAGER

THE NEW UNBLOCKED MANAGER

A PRACTICAL GUIDE TO SELF-DEVELOPMENT

DAVE FRANCIS AND MIKE WOODCOCK

Gower

First published 1982 as *The Unblocked Manager* by Gower Publishing Co Ltd
This edition published by
Gower Publishing Limited
Gower House
Croft Road
Aldershot
Hampshire GU11 3HR
England

Gower
Old Post Road
Brookfield
Vermont 05036
USA

Dave Francis and Mike Woodcock have asserted their right under the Copyright, Designs and Patents Act 1988 to be identified as the authors of this work.

British Library Cataloguing in Publication Data
Francis, Dave
   The new unblocked manager : a practical guide to
   self-development. – 2nd ed.
   1. Executive ability   2. Management
   I. Title II.   Woodcock, Mike
   658.4'09

ISBN 0–566–07639–X Hardback
ISBN 0–566–07705–1 Paperback

Library of Congress Cataloging-in-Publication Data
Francis, Dave.
   The new unblocked manager : a practical guide to self-development /
  Dave Francis and Mike Woodcock. — Rev. ed.
     p. cm.
   Rev. ed. of: The unblocked manager. 1982.
   Includes index.
   ISBN 0–566–07639–X. — ISBN 0–566–07705–1 (pbk.)
   1. Management—Study   and   teaching. 2. Self-culture. 3. Self-
evaluation. I. Woodcock, Mike. II. Francis, Dave. Unblocked manager.
III. Title.
HD30.4.F7   1996
658—dc20
                                               95–40203
                                                 CIP

Typeset in Century Schoolbook by Poole Typesetting (Wessex) Ltd and
Printed and bound in Great Britain by Hartnolls Ltd, Bodmin, Cornwall

CONTENTS

LIST OF FIGURES

PREFACE

This is unashamedly a self-help book which provides a comprehensive structure for planned, self-directed, development. Many people find the title intriguing. Why the *new unblocked* manager? Well, we believe that real development is as much to do with liberating latent talent as with acquiring new knowledge and skills. Accordingly, the structured self-help approach developed in this book concentrates on helping managers explore those factors which are holding them back and then confronting these blockages directly and intensively.

This is a second edition of a book originally published in 1982 as *The Unblocked Manager*. It seems to have achieved a measure of success, to judge from the warm reviews, the continuing sales and the fact that the text is now available in ten languages. We have fundamentally revised the material from the first edition, which naturally reflected the needs of managers in the 1980s. We have received a great deal of feedback from practising managers which provided an invaluable basis for this new edition. Our work as teachers and researchers has opened our minds to 'new paradigm concepts' and we owe a debt to the School of Management at the University of Lancaster (where Mike Woodcock is a Visiting Professor), to Leeds Business School (where Mike Woodcock is a Visiting Fellow) and to the Centre for Research in Innovation Management at the University of Brighton (where Dave Francis is undertaking research).

We hope that old friends of *The Unblocked Manager* will find that the new edition retains those techniques and ideas which have proven themselves since the book first appeared. However, much has changed in the world of management and so there is a great deal of new material. In particular, we have developed the concept of management competences which has received a great deal of attention over the past decade. In the first edition we defined a competence as 'a basis of managerial capability' rather than a list of behaviours. We continue to adopt this broad definition but, unlike many authors, we see competence as a challenge as well as a description. The key question is 'what competences will managers need in the twenty-first century?'. By answering this question we move from a description model to an approach which is dynamic, speculative and interpretive. We hope our readers accept this 'aspirational' definition of managerial competences since our aim is to develop a vision of management in tomorrow's organizations rather than simply describe best current practice.

The New Unblocked Manager is written at a time when the concept of organization (and therefore management) is being profoundly questioned. For generations we have conceptualized organizations as hierarchical machines directed by a small band of wise general managers. Deciding what to do was separated from implementation. Many organizations had rigid status differences ordered by formal rules. Each of the assumptions on which our notion of 'organization' is developed is now in question – today we find it more fruitful to see organizations as ever-changing information-rich networks in which decisions and implementation merge seamlessly within an overarching set of intentions and visions. Such basic change requires a fundamental redefinition of the term 'management'.

There are profound shifts in the context of management. The centre of gravity of many of the world's economic activities has moved to the Far East. Global competition in everything from telecommunications to education is commonplace. In many countries political and social trends reduce options and add costs. Management is a responsive craft, creating value despite a horde of potentially negative influences. It is tempting to try to avoid harsh realities but escapism is a barren philosophy. This book argues the case for a positive alternative and for relishing the struggle to thrive by being stronger and fitter.

In every situation negative and unpredictable forces are at work. No manager can relax and feel 'I've made it'. The spectre of decline, mediocrity and failure is an everyday companion.

Charles Darwin was the first to describe how species flourish through their capacity to adapt and evolve into higher life forms. This natural process is an imperative for every manager. Without a personal evolutionary process all of us lose our relevance.

The New Unblocked Manager is not a management textbook to be read and forgotten. Rather the book requires your active involvement to be effective. You will find down-to-earth and well-tested ideas which will help you become more effective, but you need to use them time and time again to make the ideas your own.

Anyone writing a book about personal development is reworking a theme continuously discussed since the Old Testament prophets first began to describe the process of enriching life through conscious development. You will find that many of our ideas are derived from others, whom we have acknowledged where possible. Our greatest debt of thanks is owed to the thousands of managers with whom we have worked over the years. Management is a 'craft' in the ancient meaning of the term. We learn from skilled practitioners and our task, as authors, is to convey the thinking of exceptionally proficient managers to a wider audience.

Dave Francis
Mike Woodcock

INTRODUCTION

Managers are everywhere. If you have a bad meal in a restaurant and want to complain you ask to see 'the manager'. Top managers have enormous power over people's lives: they open and close factories, decide whether to pollute the environment and make a huge contribution to national bank balances.

What makes a 'good' manager? This question has exercised the minds of managers and researchers over the past 100 years. Lists of desirable attributes usually fill several close-typed pages and end up looking like a specification for sainthood! A practical theory is required and the notion that an effective manager is one who is 'unblocked' is both simple and positive.

Management is a craft, like carpentry or stone carving. The manager is not a scientist, although there are many opportunities for research and the application of logic. The manager is not an artist, although passion and intuition are attributes of successful managers. Managers are practitioners – specialists in the obscure mystery of getting things done.

The manager blends art and science with accumulated experience and the wisdom of others – the attributes of a craft. Management can only be learned by achievement in the real world. Just as a potter must learn to work clay through countless hours of practice so a manager can only learn by organizing people and resources to meet a variety of objectives in a myriad of demanding situations.

This book adopts a simple but profound principle – highly successful managers must possess all the competences of their craft. Inadequately developed competences block the progress of the manager and need to be highlighted and addressed specifically. In a way this is against natural instincts since people prefer to build on their strengths. Yet it is our blockages that hold us back.

Although this book is dedicated to improving the performance and confidence of individual managers, it is important to begin by placing management within the context of today's and tomorrow's challenges.

In the next few pages we highlight key issues which are reshaping the management role – we call these 'change drivers'. From here we determine what competences managers will need to thrive in tomorrow's organizations. In the New Unblocked Manager model there are twelve key competences which managers must develop.

The twelve competences provide the basic structure for the book but the list, in itself, is sterile. Later we develop the theory of 'blockages' and this concept enables a manager to shape his or her personal development by concentrating on underdeveloped competences which require focused energy and commitment. The 'blockage' concept of self-development is our tool for transforming a list of desirable attributes into a step-by-step personal development process.

MANAGEMENT INTO THE FUTURE

The world is becoming richer. As people are able to afford more goods and services, so markets expand. However, supply is almost unrestricted and competition fearsome – only world-class organizations can win.

Each individual manager must cope intellectually and emotionally with an increasing pace of change. Information technology enables hugely complex tasks to be managed with a precision never before achieved. New organizational structures demand a high level of 'soft' skills like coaching, networking, teambuilding, negotiating and creating business. Increasing demands on managers, driven by the need to de-layer, reduce costs and increase productivity, have increased expectations and stress, stimulating some and unnerving others.

Perhaps the most significant change is growing global competition. This is vividly illustrated when we look around our homes. A typical British house may contain an Italian refrigerator, a Japanese camcorder, a German food mixer, American toilet wipes, linen from India. All managers, whether they like it of not, operate on a world stage.

External forces drive change. Individuals must adapt and thrive or opt out. Darwin's study of the dynamics of evolution is uncanny in its relevance to the management task. Each manager must adopt learning as a personal motif or risk obsolescence.

The task is made more urgent by the changing structure of managerial work. Twenty years ago the dominant change driver was mechanization, as automated equipment simplified or replaced routine manual tasks. Today automation has spread to the routine work of the mind, and so the tasks that humans perform are increasingly nonroutine and inherently challenging.

It is easy to believe that the pace of change brings more threats than benefits. Gloomy predictions about the future are often voiced. However, forecasters of doom ignore one essential human characteristic: the capacity of people to innovate and to overcome obstacles. Pessimistic viewpoints can bring about the doleful conditions they foretell. A negative downward spiral has spurious attractions as it permits the manager to justify failure. Management cannot thrive by adopting a loser mentality. A positive attitude is essential. Mountains are not climbed by sitting in a hotel contemplating the difficulties ahead.

 MANAGEMENT NEEDS

These broad trends influence the way managers must structure their development. Capabilities must be acquired to thrive in tomorrow's organizations. Let us examine in more detail the forces affecting the individual manager. Figure 1 helps us to see the 'big picture'. There are four primary change drivers.

POLITICAL, SOCIAL AND MARKET CHANGES

Trends in the way people think and feel shape consumption patterns; they are thus fundamental drivers of change. It is only necessary to reflect on the way shipbuilding has declined in Europe or the impact of social change in the former USSR to recognize the effect of social and market forces. Of particular importance is the growth of 'expectations' – the authors can recall when it was considered reasonable to wait for three months to have a telephone installed. Now a consumer would be disappointed if the phone was not installed within 48 hours.

Social changes affect management in a more direct way. The attitudes and expectations of the workforce determine how managers operate day by day. The distant formal managerial styles beloved by previous generations of managers have, increasingly, been superseded by a close, empowering stance, demanding very different skills.

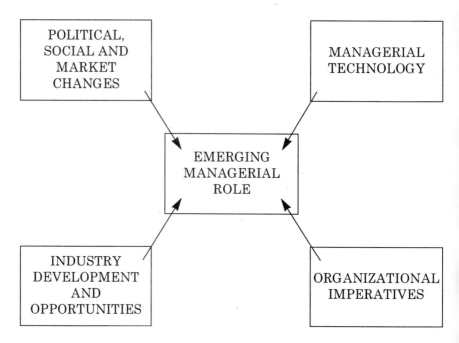

Figure 1 Primary change drivers

The influence of political forces and legislation on management practice is sometimes direct and dramatic. Political decisions can prove to be opportunities, threats or constraints. Each can affect management in a myriad of subtle ways.

Political, social and market change drivers define the context for management. Even broad trends have a direct impact. Managers need to be open to the world and find ways to relate change drivers to their own practice.

INDUSTRY DEVELOPMENT AND OPPORTUNITIES

An industry is a group of firms whose products and services are substitutes for each other. Each industry is influenced by distinct and different forces. Managers must understand and react to those specific factors which drive their own industry. For example, the management task in high fashion (where style, flair and timing are of the essence) is very different from electricity generation (where engineering, reliability and financial planning are key factors).

Deep understanding of industry change drivers is essential for success. To some extent all firms in an industry are affected by the same forces. Prudent managers can sometimes adopt a strategy which avoids hazards. Once it was believed that such decisions were solely the responsibility of the most senior directing team. Now we have learned that good ideas and, therefore, strategies can emerge from any organizational level. Every manager can make a contribution to the corporate future.

The evolution of industry-specific 'technologies' is a particularly potent driver of change. Technologies may be science-based (like digital signal processing) or discipline-based (like activity-based costing). It is becoming more important to foresee upcoming industry-specific technologies and be able to exploit them speedily and aggressively.

MANAGERIAL TECHNOLOGY

All professions have their own methodologies and core values: management is no exception. Wave after wave of innovative approaches to management are devised, enhanced and propagated. Sometimes management theories prove mere fashionable fads which quickly fade, leaving no trace. Most innovations in thinking and practice have merit and become absorbed into the managerial culture, as small elements in the emerging global technology of effective management.

These changes touch each individual manager personally, directly and extensively. Energy is squandered unless the vast majority of managers in an organization 'buy in' to new initiatives and practise new techniques seriously. Cynicism – even its more moderate bedfellow, scepticism – diminishes the power of an organization to manage the continuous flow of problems and opportunities.

There are so many managerial technologies that it is impossible to summarize them. The task is to keep the mind open to new thinking, refresh established approaches and fight against an insidious decline in performance which can accompany accumulated experience.

ORGANIZATIONAL IMPERATIVES

Organizations must concentrate on achieving a coherent strategy.[1] This requires a flow of decisions that positively align the organization behind a clear driving force. No organization can be all things – choice and commitment shape the past, present and future.

---

[1] See *Step-by-Step Competitive Strategy* by Dave Francis, Routledge, 1994 for an extended discussion of the concept of competitive strategy.

The principle of will applies whenever great things are done. If a child decides to become a professional ballet dancer then this decision will shape his/her future. Many hours will be spent in stretching, practice and study. This time cannot be spent elsewhere: a ballet-oriented mind-set must be developed. The strategy decision ('I will be a ballet dancer') affects all areas of life.[2]

As organizations need a distinct strategy, each organization must be focused, distinct and aligned. In a sense, strategy is an act of will – the shakers and movers in the organization say 'we will be the suppliers of the best sausages in Europe'. Then all processes and products must be devised to achieve this goal.

The individual manager is the link between strategy and action: he or she must translate the messages of strategy into behaviour. Consider efforts to implement Total Quality Management. An example beautifully demonstrates the need to relate strategy to action. Our international courier has a poster defining the company's positive customer care policy on the wall of the local office. It reads like a recipe for delighting the customer, but what the customer experiences is the behaviour of the hung-over, hefty clerk surrounded by stacks of despatch notes. His surly indifference renders the customer care mission poster worse than useless. Strategy and action are unconnected.

Managers must shape their behaviour within the context of what the organization needs. It is the leaders' task to excite in all employees the desire to create something of real value. Managers must find ways to transform intention into enduring reality. Just as a child cannot become a professional ballet dancer without studying music, so an organization cannot achieve its strategic intent unless managers (indeed, most employees) apply the current strategic and organization development themes which their leaders advocate.

 ## MANAGEMENT COMPETENCES

What makes a 'good' manager? At first sight there are no hard and fast rules. A manager of a rock-'n'-roll band needs different capabilities from a supervisor in a hospice. Managing in Johannesburg is different from managing in Silicon Valley. Controlling a water

---

[2.] For further discussion of the impact of strategy on careers see Dave Francis, *Managing Your Own Career*, Harper Collins, 1994.

treatment plant in Madras poses different problems from steering General Motors through the twenty-first century.

Yet, if you accept our belief that management is a craft, you will see that, despite its diverse forms, it depends on a common basis of acquired skills, particular mind-sets and appropriate attitudes. Managers learn their craft from 'masters' who blend science with art; rationality with informed intuition; accumulated experience with openness to change.

Capabilities developed by 'the manager as craftsman' enable him or her to manage. These capabilities we call 'competences', defined as 'the underlying attributes needed to perform excellently on a balanced portfolio of measures today and prepare for the changed managerial requirements of tomorrow'.

As we reflect on the factors which shape the management job recurring themes emerge, demanding attention. These, we believe, are the competences required by most managers in most situations for most of the time. We identify twelve competences:

1. *Self-management* Individual managers face increasing demands. Pressure, uncertainty and complexity can demoralize and produce psychological stress. There must be constant attention to personal well-being, efficiency and time management.

2. *Personal values* As the world becomes more complex so values and beliefs are thrown into question. Ethical considerations are much more prominent than they were. Criteria for assessing what is good and bad, right or wrong, are increasingly uncertain. But managers need a positive attitude and clear principles – these can only be achieved by clarifying personal values.

3. *Leadership* The task of management includes leadership. No longer are administrative and organizational skills sufficient. A manager needs vision, courage, persuasiveness and enthusiasm.

4. *Creativity* Since ever fewer organizations are untouched by change the management job has become increasingly creative and innovative. Transformational change and continuous improvement are expected even in the most mundane activities.

5. *Personal development* The management task is not external to the individual; self-development must be directed and managed. Emotions, attitudes and commitment are as important as mind-sets, conceptual tools and skills. Everyone needs a personal strategy for broad-based continuous learning.

6. *Problem solving and decision making* As routine tasks are automated so the manager must operate increasingly in the domain of the non-routine. He or she can learn the skills of identifying and solving problems, and improve judgement as an aid to decision making. Without these capabilities the manager is fundamentally flawed.

7. *Objective setting* Determination and commitment are the principal tools of management. Without clear aims, distinct choices and aggressive objectives organizational energy is squandered. Managers need to take great care when and where they commit resources.

8. *Management style* The management task is always connected with shaping the behaviour of others. Managers must adopt a style which engages employees, concentrates energy, develops standards, exercises appropriate control and encourages alignment.

9. *Resource management* It is a cliché that, 'the task of management is organizing people to get things done'. Yet the development and integration of resources continues to challenge managers, especially as knowledge has become one of the most significant resources. The task is always to achieve better results with fewer resources as the downward pressure on costs continues.

10. *Team development* Increasingly people are working in teams with collective responsibility for achievement. Teamwork must be effective, stressing proper allocation of tasks, control, coordination and communication. The manager must become skilled at leading groups through all the trials and tribulations of development so that they emerge as resourceful and dedicated teams.

11. *People development* The best managers develop people's latent abilities. No longer can the manger regard human assets as fixed and immutable. Good managers believe that everyone has latent abilities, and become coaches, trainers, developers and educators, in addition to their managerial role.

12. *Customer focus* Every person working in a firm has 'customers' – people who use their goods or services. Sometimes these are external, for example buyers, but often customers are internal. An approach which focuses on identifying customer needs and providing wanted goods and services integrates the manager into the organization.

 MANAGERIAL BLOCKAGES

We define a *blockage* as 'a factor which inhibits the potential and output of a system (this may be a total organization, a work team or an individual)'.

Blockages are best understood by imagining a plumbing system.

Suppose water started bubbling up through your floorboards. There could be several reasons: a leak, fracture, overflow etc. Your plumber's task is to ignore those parts of the system which are working, find the blockage and put it right.

For many years educators have not followed the philosophy of your plumber: they have believed in building on strengths. While this has merit, in this book we favour the opposite view. If a manager is a great teambuilder but a poor problem solver, we argue that he/she should concentrate on his/her problem-solving skills rather than hone an already sharp skill as a teambuilder. The blockage concept says 'find those things that are holding you back, overcome your negative feelings and remove the blockages'.

All managers have the potential to develop and expand their effectivenes. The fastest and most economical way to bring about rapid self-development is to explore, understand and overcome blockages which are inhibiting success and personal growth.

It makes sense to focus attention on factors that are inhibiting the full achievement of potential. The twelve blockages which we use as the framework for this book provide a vehicle for self-assessment and action planning. The categories are not meant to be complete (they relate to generic management skills rather than technical disciplines) but they apply widely, and the new definitions have evolved from the views of thousands of managers who have used earlier versions of this book.

 ## THE UNBLOCKED MANAGER COMPETENCY MODEL

We assert that managers must have the following:
1. Competent self-management
2. Sound personal values
3. Impressive leadership vision
4. High creativity
5. An active approach to self-development
6. A structured approach to problem solving and decision making
7. An effective process for objective setting
8. A positive management style
9. Good organizing skills
10. A strong team-development capability
11. A dynamic approach to people development
12. A strong customer focus.

Each of these headings must be defined, explored and considered: this will be done in the remainder of the book. However, the list is central to the unblocking theory: our argument is that every manager needs each of these attributes. If one or more are absent the chain is broken, and personal efficiency and effectiveness are weakened.

DEVELOPING PERSONAL COMPETENCES

Turbulent times affect organizations generally but have their most immediate impact on individuals. For the individual manager this could mean that his/her standard of living is eroded, his/her development potential is neglected, or, perhaps, he/she may have no worthwhile work to do at all. It is, therefore, in every manager's personal interest to invest time and energy in sustaining a high level of personal effectiveness. This is the most reliable insurance against the risks associated with managerial life.

Social systems limit individual opportunities by valuing certain contributions more highly than others. However, except in profoundly sick or tyrannical regimes, individuals can influence their own futures and be the principal determinants of the quality of their own lives. The ability to choose and influence one's own future is, perhaps, an individual's most precious asset but few people appear to fully capitalize on their opportunities. Their lives are limited by constraints which accident, history, and commitment impose.

Being in charge of one's own life has been well described as self-responsibility, and it is fundamental to the approach espoused in this book. From experience we know that people do not become self-responsible rapidly or easily.

As organizational life becomes more demanding and uncertain, better managers are needed. Individual managers must become more personally resourceful by learning to take a greater responsibility for themselves, their careers, and their potential. Self-responsibility increases the individual manager's usefulness, drive, and capacity to survive, and the organization gains a resource that will continue to be valuable in the future.

An organization requires relevant and effective contributions from all its managers but cannot by itself bring about the development of every managerial skill in every manager. Even if this were possible, it would be an excessive use of resources. Both the organization and the individual have a part to play in developing management competence.

It is helpful for managers and supervisors to take a coherent and systematic approach to their development. Once professional skills are mastered, they form a solid base for competent performance. In developing our model, we have tried to incorporate new research findings drawn from behavioural science and to express them in a jargon-free and comprehensible manner. However, we are more concerned with practice than with conceptual elegance and it is through the comments of practising managers that we have been able to develop our most useful techniques. We have avoided being tentative when we believe we are on the right track, and our suggestions are partisan. We assume that as you read this book you will adopt only those ideas that make sense to you for your situation.

We have designed this book so that you will derive the maximum benefit from it. Following this Introduction, you will be invited in Part I to make a preliminary examination of your own personal blockages. Part II contains twelve chapters, each explaining one of the blockages we have outlined. Taken together, these chapters constitute an integrated philosophy of managing people that is relevant now and in the future. Because many of the ideas are interconnected, we ask you to read Part II in full. Some of the ideas in it may be familiar to you and others will be new. Both the old and the new can be combined to give you a foundation for assessing your managerial strengths and your developmental needs.

Part III offers an additional survey that will give you feedback from others – a report of how they see your blockages. Your assessment of your own blockages will, therefore, become more accurate and your development plans will stand a better chance of success.

The book is designed to be used in a flexible way. For example, after completing the later survey you can return to Part II and re-read the sections that most apply to you. Our approach emphasizes experimentation and learning from experience. As you work on clearing your blockages, you can use the surveys to monitor your progress.

We suggest that you undertake the personal assessment, Blockage Survey (Self) in Part I, as soon as possible and before reading the chapters on each of the blockages. The insights gained from reading the blockage chapters could prejudice your results on the survey.

The additional survey in Part III has been placed there because it provides new information that is better used after you have explored the main premises of the blockage model. You may choose to complete the assessments in Part III before reading the chapters in Part II.

The material in this book has been designed principally for individuals but can be used as the basis for a self-directed management development programme sponsored by an organization or business school. Whichever way *The New Unblocked Manager* is used it will, hopefully, provoke, clarify, enrich and enlighten.

ASSESSING YOUR PERSONAL BLOCKAGES

THE BLOCKAGE SURVEY (SELF)

The changing patterns and requirements of management have been examined and now it is time to take stock of your own capacities as a manager or supervisor. To do this, we invite you to complete the Blockage Survey (Self), which will help you to identify your strengths and personal blockages. By assessing yourself before reading further, you can gain useful feedback and be able to use the blockage chapters in Part II more purposefully.

 USING THE BLOCKAGE SURVEY (SELF)

PURPOSE

To provide a framework for systematically assessing personal strengths and blockages to managing effectively.

TIME

Approximately twenty minutes to complete the survey, followed by forty minutes for reflection or discussion.

MATERIALS

The survey is set out on the next few pages, but the answer sheet may be photocopied if you do not want to mark your book.[1]

SETTING

It is important not to rush completion, so choose a quiet place where you can work undisturbed.

METHOD

1. Read the instructions before you complete the survey.
2. Try to consider each statement separately and leave analysis until the end of the survey.
3. When you have completed the survey, consider the results carefully in order to assess how valid they are for you.

A NOTE OF CAUTION

Although the survey is methodical and logical, it reflects your subjective views and it should therefore be seen as an aid to self-review rather than as a scientific measure. Later in the book we invite you to collect data to assess the relevance and objectivity of your conclusions.

---

[1] This instrument is the copyright of Challenge Ltd, from whom additional copies may be obtained. Contact Challenge Ltd, Challenge House, 45/47 Victoria Street, Mansfield, Notts. NG18 5SU. Tel.: 01623 645901. Fax: 01623 22621.

THE BLOCKAGE SURVEY (SELF)

INSTRUCTIONS FOR COMPLETING THE SURVEY

This survey will help you to clarify your own development needs.

As you score the questionnaire reflect on:

— your current abilities compared with excellent performers in jobs similar to yours

— the new competencies that your job will require in three years time

— capabilities that you need for your career plan.

On the following pages you will find five sections. Complete each section in the same way.

For each section you have 20 points which *must* be allocated. Look over the list of twelve items and allocate the points to represent your personal development needs. One item can receive all twenty points, or you can spread the points over as many items as you wish – the aim is to highlight your own development needs.

SECTION ONE

Allocate 20 points between these twelve items.

In my job, I need to do these things more or better . . .

	1.	maintain a high level of personal energy	
	2.	know where I stand on matters of principle	
	3.	have a clear 'vision' of what needs to be done	
5	4.	provide creative ideas ✓	
	5.	take my own development seriously	10
8	6.	solve problems in a structured way ✓	5
8	7.	set clear goals for others	5
3	8.	motivate those who work for me ✓	
3	9.	manage projects efficiently ✓	
3	10.	build high-performing teams ✓	
3	11.	create opportunities to help others to develop ✓	
	12.	focus on satisfying customers (internal or external)	

SECTION TWO

Allocate 20 points between these twelve items.

I need to improve these activities . . .

13. seeking outside assessments of my group's efficiency $_\vee$ [ ]

14. holding regular coaching sessions with my staff $_\vee$ [ ]

15. leading teams towards achieving shared objectives [ ]

16. making better use of available resources [ ]

17. taking a firm line with low-performing people [5]

18. running productive meetings $_\vee$ $_{\text{my}}$ [5]

19. developing a wider range of options before taking a decision $_\vee$ [ ]

20. setting time aside for my own learning [5]

21. suggesting radical ways to improve processes [ ]

22. obtaining other people's commitment to objectives [ ]

23. dealing confidently with decisions that involve finely-balanced value judgements [ ]

24. managing my own time efficiently [5]

SECTION THREE

Allocate 20 points between these twelve items.

I would perform better if I . . .

8 ✓ 25.   reduced my personal stress level   [6]

26.   operated from a coherent 'philosophy' of management   [ ]

27.   enrolled others to support my initiatives   [ ]

6 ✓ 28.   suggested more innovative ideas   [ ]

29.   set demanding development objectives for myself   [ ]

30.   took more time for decision making when issues are
important   [5]

31.   measured other people's performance objectively   [2]

6 ✓ 32.   gave greater emotional support to others   [ ]

33.   delegated effectively   [2]

34.   developed a more positive climate in teams   [5]

35.   gave counselling to my staff   [ ]

36.   worked co-operatively with other departments
and teams   [ ]

SECTION FOUR

Allocate 20 points between these twelve items.

I would be a more skilful manager if I . . .

37. sought regular feedback about performance from internal or external customers ☐
38. actively provided opportunities for staff to develop their abilities ☐
39. helped work groups to clarify their team development needs ☐ *5*
40. designed effective work processes ☐
41. communicated systematically to my staff ☐
42. ensured that key objectives are measured ☐ *5*
43. consciously involved others in decision making ☐ *5*
44. tried new ideas to extend my experience ☐
45. seized opportunities that others miss ☐
46. enrolled others in my vision of what needs to be done ☐
47. fundamentally questioned my own values from time to time ☐
48. dealt with setbacks without losing confidence ☐ *5*

SECTION FIVE

Allocate 20 points between these twelve items.

My own development needs are to . . .

49. maintain a higher level of energy

50. behave in ways that are more consistent with my beliefs

51. be more assertive

52. maintain effort when solutions cannot be readily found

53. learn from honest feedback on my own strengths and weaknesses

54. handle complex information with clarity and confidence

55. monitor progress towards the achievement of goals

56. supervise others according to their individual needs

57. organize people and resources efficiently

58. develop high-performing teams

59. appraise comprehensively the performance of subordinates

60. developing a clear understanding of my customers' (internal or external) needs

ANSWER GRID FOR THE BLOCKAGE SURVEY (SELF)

Copy the number for each of the five sections onto the answer grid below and add the scores for each horizontal line.

Totals

1	24	25	48	49		
		8			8	1
2	23	26	47	50		
						2
3	22	27	46	51		
						3
4	21	28	45	52		
5		6			11	4
5	20	29	44	53		
						5
6	17	30	43	54		
	3			10	13	6
7	18	31	42	55		
	8			16	18	7
8	17	32	41	56		
3		6	6		15	8
9	16	33	40	57		
3			8		11	9
10	15	34	39	58		
3			6		9	10
11	14	35	38	59		
3	4				7	11
12	13	36	37	60		
	3				3	12

Now transfer the numbers to the next page.

SCORING SHEET FOR THE BLOCKAGES SURVEY (SELF)

INSTRUCTIONS

1. Enter the total from the answer grid sheet for each of the 12 categories in the *Your score* column.
2. Fill in the *Ranking* column by giving your highest score a ranking of 1, the second highest score a ranking of 2 and continue. Your lowest score is ranked 12.

	YOUR SCORE	RANKING	BLOCKAGE
1	8		Incompetent self-management
2			Negative personal values
3			Inferior leadership vision
4	11		Low creativity
5			Passive personal development
6	13		Unstructured problem solving and decision making
7	18		Unclear goals
8	15		Negative management style
9	11		Poor organizing skills
10	9		Weak team-building capacity
11	7		Inactive people development
12	5		Weak customer focus

WHAT DO THE SCORES MEAN?

Your highest scores represent possible blockages to achieving your management potential. We suggest that you take the three or four highest scores and explore them further. Read the summary notes below, decide which blockages you want to work on and read the relevant blockage essays in the next section of this book.

THE 12 BLOCKAGES

1. *Incompetent self-management* Being unable to make the most of one's time, energy and skills; being unable to cope with the stresses of managerial life.
2. *Negative personal values* Being unclear about one's own values; having values that are inappropriate to leading and managing. Not striving to be a responsible manager.
3. *Inferior leadership vision* Not having a coherent vision of what should be done. Being unable to engage others in the realization of a vision.
4. *Low creativity* Lacking the capacity to generate new ideas, failing to capitalize on ideas and lacking skills in innovation management.
5. *Passive personal development* Taking a passive attitude to the development of competence and neglecting self-development.
6. *Unstructured problem solving and decision making* Lacking effective strategies and techniques for problem solving and decision making.
7. *Unclear goals* Lacking a goal-oriented approach to management and not focusing energy on the achievement of objectives.
8. *Negative management style* Being ineffective in motivating, supporting and directing people.
9. *Poor organizing skills* Lacking the capacity to find, organize, exploit and use resources effectively.
10. *Weak teambuilding capacity* Ineffective at integrating individuals into high-performing teams.
11. *Inactive people development* Lacking the ability or willingness to help others to grow and expand their capabilities.
12. *Weak customer focus* Not taking a vigorous customer-oriented approach.

BLOCKAGES TO PERSONAL EFFECTIVENESS

INTRODUCTION TO THE BLOCKAGES

In Part I you used the Blockage Survey to assess what might be preventing you from managing more effectively. In particular you were asked to identify three personal blockages. Part II will help you explore your blockages further. 'Know your enemy' is the rule because the first step toward self-improvement is to understand what is inhibiting your development as a manager.

Each chapter of Part II discusses one of the twelve blockages and suggests how to clear them. The key concepts and ideas are summarized here.

BLOCKAGE 1   INCOMPETENT SELF-MANAGEMENT

- ❏ Maintaining physical health
- ❏ Using energy well
- ❏ Coping with pressure
- ❏ Stress management
- ❏ Using time effectively
- ❏ 'Dualling' – making the most of time and opportunity
- ❏ When managers most need self-management competence

BLOCKAGE 2   NEGATIVE PERSONAL VALUES

- ❏ What are values?
- ❏ Choices about values

- ❑   The acquisition of values
- ❑   Life positions
- ❑   Active and passive managers
- ❑   How to clarify and change values
- ❑   Managerial values
- ❑   When managers most need positive personal values

BLOCKAGE 3   INFERIOR MANAGEMENT VISION

- ❑   Creating a leadership vision
- ❑   Influencing others
- ❑   Personal assertion
- ❑   Barriers to effective assertion
- ❑   Improving personal relationships
- ❑   Leading others
- ❑   Influencing groups and organizations
- ❑   Developing listening skills
- ❑   When managers most need leadership skills

BLOCKAGE 4   LOW CREATIVITY

- ❑   Barriers to personal creativity
- ❑   Creative problem solving
- ❑   Exploring problems
- ❑   Generating ideas
- ❑   Screening ideas
- ❑   Managing for innovation
- ❑   Feedback and review
- ❑   Creative groups and organizations
- ❑   Managing creative groups
- ❑   Personal creativity
- ❑   When managers most need to be creative

BLOCKAGE 5   PASSIVE PERSONAL DEVELOPMENT

- ❑ What is personal development?
- ❑ Common blockages to realizing potential
- ❑ Increasing personal insight
- ❑ Effective feedback
- ❑ Developing openness and flexibility
- ❑ Professional and career development
- ❑ Passive personal development as a blockage
- ❑ When managers most need personal development

BLOCKAGE 6   UNSTRUCTURED PROBLEM SOLVING AND DECISION MAKING

- ❑ Structured problem solving
- ❑ Problem-solving techniques
- ❑ Levels of decision making
- ❑ Decision-making processes
- ❑ Using people and resources to solve problems
- ❑ When managers most need problem-solving and decision-making skills

BLOCKAGE 7   UNCLEAR GOALS

- ❑ Goal setting: an attitude towards life
- ❑ Principals of effective goal setting
- ❑ Why set goals for yourself?
- ❑ How to set goals for yourself?
- ❑ Reviewing progress
- ❑ Helping others to set goals
- ❑ Impediments to effective objectives
- ❑ When managers most need clear goals

BLOCKAGE 8   NEGATIVE MANAGEMENT STYLE

- ❑ Corporate management philosophies
- ❑ Building positive work climates
- ❑ Personal energy in organizations
- ❑ Common barriers to motivation
- ❑ Motivation conditioners and key motivators
- ❑ Individual managerial insight
- ❑ The development of leadership theory
- ❑ Current leadership ideas
- ❑ Situational leadership
- ❑ The leader's personality
- ❑ When managers most need positive management style

BLOCKAGE 9   POOR ORGANIZING SKILLS

- ❑ The managerial role
- ❑ Analysing your role
- ❑ Pressures on managers
- ❑ Defining people's jobs
- ❑ Delegating responsibility
- ❑ Rewarding effective performance
- ❑ Resource allocation
- ❑ Planning and scheduling
- ❑ When managers most need effective organizing skills

BLOCKAGE 10   WEAK TEAMBUILDING CAPACITY

- ❑ Recognizing the potential of teambuilding
- ❑ The role of the team leader
- ❑ Establishing teambuilding priorities
- ❑ The teambuilder's charter
- ❑ Effective team leader style
- ❑ Developing team maturity

- ☐ The stages of team development
- ☐ When managers most need teambuilding skills

BLOCKAGE 11   INACTIVE PEOPLE DEVELOPMENT

- ☐ Training as a key management task
- ☐ The manager as a part-time trainer
- ☐ Creating a climate for personal growth
- ☐ Developing craftsmanship as a manager
- ☐ Characteristics of a positive learning climate
- ☐ Assessing individual training needs
- ☐ Conducting appraisal interviews
- ☐ Developing counselling skills
- ☐ Counselling opportunities
- ☐ Guidelines for giving effective feedback
- ☐ Learning from work experience
- ☐ Learning new tasks
- ☐ Coaching skills
- ☐ When managers most need high trainer capability

BLOCKAGE 12   WEAK CUSTOMER FOCUS

- ☐ Who is a customer?
- ☐ Defining stakeholders
- ☐ Identifying customer needs
- ☐ Contracting
- ☐ Being customer-oriented
- ☐ When managers most need customer focus

We suggest that you read the blockage essays, that you think may be relevant for you but remember that the Blockage Survey (Self) represents only your subjective assessment of yourself. This is valuable but it may not be completely accurate. In Part III there is another method that you can use to increase the accuracy of the assessment. The Blockage Survey (Other) offers you an opportunity to collect other people's evaluations of your capability and to contrast their views with your own.

Now you may choose:

1. To examine the blockage essays immediately, bearing in mind the possibly biased results and subjectivity of the Blockage Survey (Self); or

2. To turn to Part III and collect feedback from others using the Blockage Survey (Other) before reading about the blockages.

BLOCKAGE

1

INCOMPETENT SELF-MANAGEMENT

The factory was not performing well. Profitability was low. International competition, worldwide recession and a declining home market had eroded competitiveness. George Smith, the general manager, worked frenetically for all the hours he could, arriving early, staying late, taking work home and rushing from one meeting to another in a frenzy of managerial activity. Each evening he would return home to shuffle papers and write reports, eventually slumping exhausted in front of the television while dozing over an article in a management journal. Although he planned holidays with his wife, he almost always cancelled them to cope with another 'crisis'. His wife at first had become angry at the extent of George's job commitment but, failing to influence his behaviour, she lapsed into sullen resentment.

George's work became increasingly haphazard and he spent endless hours on trivia. He was pallid and overweight, and he tapped his fingers on any convenient surface. He smoked incessantly and allowed his suits to become stained and worn.

George's consuming passion was management and he devoted his few leisure hours to lecturing student groups on management topics. Once he overhead himself described as a 'workaholic type', but he dismissed the observation as a shallow remark from an irresponsible and weak colleague. One close associate said, 'George gives too much and he takes no nourishment for himself. I'm afraid that he will crack up'. It came as no surprise to George's colleagues when they heard that he was in hospital after a heart attack.

George was fortunate; he recovered and returned to his job. But he adopted a new attitude toward life and work. He said, 'I still want to work and to achieve but I'm not going to drive myself like a machine. I'm ashamed of having neglected myself'. The experience of nearly losing his life had taught George to care for himself in a new way.

 ## WHY EVERY MANAGER NEEDS SELF-MANAGEMENT

A managerial job holds many attractions. Managers have influence and power. Their decisions shape people's lives. They can take opportunities to develop skills and to relish new challenges. The role of manager has esteem and significance. Many managers find their jobs exciting and rewarding. However, if organizational processes and events unfolded in a straightforward and planned way, there would be little need for managers at all. The manager's role invariably involves working on difficult problems and choosing between uncertain options. Tension is implicit and the manager frequently feels stressed.

Organizations are greedy for human energy and can drain their managers of their spontaneity, creativity and enjoyment of life. Some people can manage themselves well despite pressures and difficulties, while others succumb to stress, exhaustion, demoralization and even disease. There is a saying that 'the cobbler's sons are often the worst shod' and managers often fail to look after themselves with the same care they devote to achieving business objectives.

This lack of care for well-being has many negative effects. The quality of decision making is affected by stress levels. As tension increases biochemical changes occur which are linked with illogical or unwise decision making. Individual managers, such as George Smith, can become so preoccupied with the importance of their jobs that they undermine their own health and vitality while serving the voracious needs of their organization.

Managerial self-neglect leads to serious long-term effects. There is a risk of deteriorating health, fractured family relationships, increasing anxiety, personal unhappiness and ineffective performance. As George Smith learned, preventing self-destruction calls for effective self-management. Before we can manage others we must first be able to manage ourselves.

It would be wrong to claim that all stress is harmful. Insufficient challenge can be as destructive as excessive pressure. The aim is to keep personal stress levels between understimulation and excessive demand.

 ## WHAT IS SELF-MANAGEMENT?

This section could easily be titled 'The Care and Maintenance of the Manager' because it suggests how a person can thrive while coping with the often excessive demands of managerial life. Because self-management is complex, it is helpful to explore the characteristics of a manager who manages himself well. Add anything you consider important to your own well-being to the following list:

❑   A healthy body
❑   Absence of damaging personal habits
❑   Energy and vitality
❑   A relaxed and balanced approach to life and work
❑   Ability to deal with overload and stress
❑   Effective use of time.

All aspects of self-management are interrelated, but for convenience, we shall explore the topic from five points of view: maintaining physical health; using energy well; coping with pressure; using time well; and maintaining balance.

MAINTAINING PHYSICAL HEALTH

There was a time when anyone known to be taking strenuous exercise would be the target for disparaging remarks from portly gentlemen puffing cigarettes over their gin and tonics. Today's managers are much more aware of the need to be physically fit. The fashion has changed and it has become almost an embarrassment to admit that one does not play tennis, swim, jog, pump iron or power-walk. So much has been written about various sports and exercise routines that it would be repetitious to mention them here. However, our practical experience and observations of managers who manage themselves competently have convinced us that the following principles make sense.

Watch your weight

A successful and busy manager has plenty of opportunity to eat too well and drink too much. All those nights dozing in Club Class seats while cruising from one continent to another can make the manager feel like a confined goose being forcibly fed for exotic paté. If you are overweight, then it is an important priority for you to find a healthy pattern of eating and drinking. Of course, there are many organizations, books and individuals that offer guidance and training in the self-management of eating and drinking. The greatest help comes from the support of others as you embark on the unpleasant process of becoming smaller. You must submit to discipline, take a pride in abstinence and adopt the stoical principle of accepting tribulation as a normal part of life's experience.

Take some exercise that you enjoy

Our bodies are made to work and without use they degenerate. A manager should exercise regularly and frequently. However, experience teaches us that without a sense of enjoyment and accomplishment, it is tedious to sustain an exercise pattern. You will, therefore, want to involve yourself in activities that meet your needs for pleasure as well as maintain your physical health.

Balance your life activities

Some activities drain energy and others nurture it. The pattern is different for each individual. For example, some people are energized by socializing whilst others find it draining. Because health is a matter of balance, it is important for managers not to allow their activities to become too one-sided. Find activities that together provide a full and varied life pattern. Holidays are vital because they provide opportunities that simply cannot be found in the normal pattern of a busy life.

Beware of unhealthy habits

Managers are subject to commonplace addictions. The most familiar are alcohol consumption and smoking. Whilst we argue that a glass or two of wine a day is the cleaning agent for the blood, excessive drinking and smoking are, of course, hazardous to health and the risks are enlarged with increased consumption. Many heavy cigarette smokers are preoccupied with the need to 'give it up' but the difficulty is knowing how to break a long-standing habit. It is a principle of self-management competence to learn control of one's own behaviour. This means strengthening willpower: the capacity to take charge of all the different mood states that we experience involves attempting to break unhelpful habits and, in the process, understanding more about ourselves.

Travel intelligently

Many managers move about the world a great deal and this is physically demanding. Because travel can be uniquely exhausting it is wise when travelling to take a miserly attitude toward your own energy. Once you have established that the journey is necessary, ask yourself, 'What is the least exhausting, most time-saving, productive and enjoyable way to make the journey?' Then give yourself the opportunity to sleep, exercise and play.

Our experience in discussing self-management with managers has shown us that the principles outlined above are readily accepted but that change is much harder to accomplish. One manager put it this way: 'It's all very well talking about health but the most important thing is for the individual to be really concerned about his own welfare. If you are not interested in yourself, then all the good advice in the world will be like water rolling off a duck's back.'

Learn to love yourself and become economical with commitments. The most productive people get to know themselves, and treat themselves with kindness and respect. Ultimately the person is more important than the job.

USING ENERGY WELL

Personal energy is a capacity to experience, develop and achieve. Energy is a primary tool for managers since those things you pay attention to are those that get done. People vary greatly in their energy levels, but few realize that energy can be managed. For some people, energy is seen as a finite resource like fuel in an automobile: when the fuel is consumed, there is no more power. Personal energy is more complicated than that, as people can manage their energy levels.

Generally a person's energy level declines with age. Some individuals, whatever their age, dissipate their energies while others retain an energetic and creative involvement in life through all their years. Such observations indicate that human energy has psychological as well as physical sources. Each of us must embark on a journey of self-understanding to find those fears, disappointments and hurts that have become inner blockages, and allow them to be expressed and discharged. The vitality of an individual is diminished or increased by emotional history.

ENERGY AND EMOTION

Psychological energy can be used positively and constructively or negatively and harmfully. You can undermine the effectiveness of others by suppressing or denying their energy and you can block your own effectiveness by suppressing or denying your own feelings.

Some people are unable or unwilling to come to terms with their feelings. They reject emotion as 'a nuisance' – an unwelcome intrusion in the business world. Since they consider emotion and expression of feelings to be a weakness, such people would like to become both less emotional and less emotive. They see some emotions as 'negative' and would like to eliminate them from their lives, for example anger, fear, jealousy, self-doubt and vulnerability. The emotions they may accept and the reasons they find them positive include the following:

❑   *Excitement* – because it stimulates activity
❑   *Compassion* – because it permits humane relationships
❑   *Interest* – because it helps progress
❑   *Curiosity* – because it probes new areas
❑   *Confidence* – because it adds weight and style to one's endeavours.

In summary, some people want the world to be a 'nice' place and deny the baser emotions. Yet there is much energy in the 'darker' side of people. Mature individuals value all their feelings and are able, for example, to express disappointment or anger. Those who try to avoid their true feelings prevent themselves from discharging the inevitable tensions that occur in life. By repressing a real part of themselves, they undermine their self-respect because they have chosen to create an image rather than confront their feelings honestly.

It is quite possible for a manager to be gifted in identifying and resolving problems, yet be flawed emotionally. This can be a severe handicap because we believe the functions of leadership and management are best performed by emotionally mature people. Observation shows us that many managers are frenetic, unstable, driven and egocentric. These qualities may produce exceptional performance but increase the risk of huge error. To respond with assertiveness, energy and creativity demands emotional maturity, which enables a manager to take the lead, confront demanding situations, cope effectively, feel good about his/her own contribution and learn how to improve next time.

Learning how to use energy effectively and to increase it is a complex endeavour but we can offer you some guidelines that have helped us.

Strive for personal insight

Energy and strength are often diminished by two factors in personality. First, a manager who suppresses self-expression may, in an effort to behave appropriately rather than honestly, curtail natural assertiveness. Second, a manager's energy may be blocked by unresolved issues related to early life. Much can be done to explore the impact of childhood experiences and free the individual to live in the present rather than the past.

Encourage self-expression

It is difficult to overestimate the importance of self-expression for maintaining a person's health and energy. Feelings need to be experienced, acknowledged and expressed. Without adequate self-expression a person may become demoralized without understanding why. For this person, effective relations with others are inhibited, achievement is stunted and the enjoyment of life is reduced.

Work for close personal relationships

Contact with others is a natural and effective way to dispel tensions, to gain support and to achieve a balanced perspective. For most people, some of the deepest feelings are felt in relation to others and close personal relationships nurture an energetic attitude toward life.

Seek challenge

Achievement despite difficulties usually increases the capacity of people to use their energies creatively. Many individuals thrive on overcoming difficulties and on 'winning' despite setbacks. On the other hand, when challenge is excessive and the individual fails, he/she may feel exhausted and demoralized. Managers need to choose assignments that will stretch capacities but not break them.

Accept failure and learn from it

It seems inevitable that people will make errors and believe that they have failed, perhaps remembering the failures with deep regret. However, failures provide opportunities for us to learn directly about ourselves and to improve what we do in the future. A risk-free life without failures demonstrates that the person is excessively cautious. Acceptance of failure is a necessary part of human experience.

Acknowledge personal worth

Managers need to cultivate a realistic, but optimistic, attitude towards themselves. Because negative attitudes towards the self do exist, they should be recognized – but positive feelings of personal worth should be given direct expression. An energetic and positive approach to life includes a celebration of accomplishment and managers should seek ways to value themselves.

Many of us need to break habitual patterns and teach ourselves to function at a higher level of energy. Much can be done by allowing yourself to express and trust your own excitement, interests and feelings. Factors that block you can then be more clearly identified and removed.

COPING WITH PRESSURE

People respond very differently to pressure. While one person may be highly disturbed by the loss of a watch, another can cope with a major international crisis without feeling overwhelmed.

Doctors are interested in individual responses to pressure and have done a great deal of research into the human stress reaction. Several of the indices of stress and tension are continuing to increase, particularly illnesses related to personal stress. In many Western communities, one person in five will, at some time in their life, need medical help for a psychological illness.

The word 'stress' is most often used to describe an experience of anxiety which combines with physiological effects such as shallow breathing and increased muscular tension. The body reacts to overstimulation and there are changes in the pattern of mental activity. Excessively stressed individuals become increasingly vulnerable to everyday pressures and their work quality deteriorates. In extreme cases of stress, an individual may behave erratically or simply give up and mentally withdraw. However, it is helpful to recognize that stress is a reaction that occurs within an individual and to some extent it can be managed.

From another viewpoint, stress is valuable because it stimulates activity. This becomes obvious when we examine how élite forces are trained in the armed services. Gruelling night expeditions, real danger, constant pressure and almost impossible challenges are essential to train soldiers to be members of élite battalions. Without such pressure the special capabilities needed would not be developed.

Insufficient stimulation and inadequate challenge can also provoke personal problems. People need a level of stimulation to give them a reason for commitment and many produce their most valuable work when under some pressure. There is evidence that insufficient tension can result in deteriorating morale, lower effectiveness and lack of self-worth. The ideal is to have sufficient challenge to stimulate achievement but not excessive demands. For example, what kind of ski instructor should you choose? A highly demanding and ruthless instructor is likely to provoke fear and withdrawal but a lazy instructor will provide insufficient challenge. The beginner on the ski slopes needs a degree of instruction, challenge and support that results in a healthy level of tension and encourages skill development.

Different human responses to the same potentially stressful situations have caused researchers to inquire into the reasons why some individuals are less stressed than others when the external demand is exactly the same. People who are relatively free from stress-related problems have adopted a lifestyle that enables them to cope easily with the demands made on them. From our observation, the following characteristics are typical of those who manage stress most successfully:

1. They shelve problems until they can deal with them. People who experience high stress often cannot let go and continue to churn over problems, worrying about likely and unlikely possibilities.

2. They deliberately relax in order to refresh the body and mind after the physical and mental demands of coping with stress. This often involves a change of activity, for example, doing some vigorous physical activity or quietly going through a planned relaxation routine.

3. They can take a wide view of the events in their lives and do not become submerged in the details of a situation.

4. They manage to control the build-up and pace of stressful situations by realistically planning and intervening to prevent themselves from being overwhelmed. They have a clear vision of the likely course of events and do not give up when problems arise.

5. They deal with problems directly and are prepared to confront difficulties or unpleasant issues.

6. They know their own capacities and do not allow themselves to be stretched excessively. They know that an appropriate level of challenge is constructive and exciting but that excessive challenge is risky and should only be taken on consciously for a limited period of time.

7. They do not wallow in negative states of depression but prefer to find the cause of a problem and then tackle it. This often involves expressing feelings openly and skilfully, working through any difficulties that occur.

8. They can cope with being unpopular. Some people who are highly affected by stress squander much of their energy being troubled about others' perceptions of them. Those who manage stress well are not excessively disturbed if other people disapprove of them.

9. They do not commit themselves to extremely tight schedules that are unlikely to be met. This is a professional attitude, and it results in not having to struggle, continuously, to meet almost impossible commitments.

10. They actively limit their involvement in work. They are prepared to devote a substantial effort to achievement but they maintain a balanced lifestyle.

These characteristics are partly personal attitudes and partly skills. The most significant are the capacity to review objectively the demands of work and to be active in solving difficult problems as they occur. Some people find this easier to accomplish by using relaxation techniques. The principle of these techniques is to become aware of one's inner processes and deliberately bring a state of relaxation into thinking and feeling. Relaxation techniques revitalize the body and quiet the mind in a surprisingly short time.

USING TIME WELL

Some managers accomplish a great deal of work within a limited time, while others constantly complain that they are unable to achieve results because of a 'shortage of time'. Fortunately all managers can learn to use time more effectively and intelligently.

A study of the effective use of time begins with developing an awareness of where your time goes. Without a full understanding of how you operate from day to day, there is no foundation for change. When you begin to examine how your time is being used, it is likely that you will make some of the following assessments:

❑   I allow my time to be used by others.
❑   I fritter away time on trivialities and less important issues.
❑   I permit my emotional reactions to misuse my time.
❑   I fail to plan sufficiently well.
❑   I do things that could be done by others.
❑   I fail to achieve important targets.

The way we use our time is a statement about who we are. The factors that reduce the effective use of time are the same as those that undermine general effectiveness.

The key to improving use of time is awareness. Consider the following example. Jack has been persuaded to go ice-skating with his adolescent children. Never having been on the ice before, he decides to take lessons. His first instructor constantly gives directions, corrects errors, and tries to teach a uniform style. For his second lesson, Jack has a different instructor who concentrates on helping him see what happens when he performs certain movements. This instructor asks questions such as the following:

❑   How does it feel to go fast?
❑   What do your feet do when you turn?
❑   How does your breathing change as you try to speed up?
❑   What happened when you fell?
❑   What are you telling yourself about your ability?

The second instructor was helping Jack to discover the effects of different movements and to learn from a heightened awareness of what was happening to him. This gave feedback about the experience rather than teaching through rigid instruction. The increased awareness enabled Jack to be the master of his learning rather than a powerless trainee.

Observing how your time is being spent and discovering whether your investment of time is meeting your needs can be done by asking yourself questions to heighten your awareness:

❑   How does it feel when I use time in different ways?
❑   What principles do I use to manage my own time?
❑   What is successful about my management of time?
❑   What is thieving my time at the moment?
❑   How efficient am I in managing time?
❑   When am I the master of time and when am I the servant?

Notice that these questions simply ask for information, not judgements. If you become dissatisfied and judge yourself negatively, then your self-judgement could inhibit your learning and change. It is more fruitful to simply notice how you spend your time and collect your own observations. These gradually influence how you view yourself and change occurs naturally. We repeat: the key to this kind of observation and learning is self-awareness.

MANAGERIAL TIME AND ENERGY

Managers and supervisors often have difficulties in allocating time: there are many demands and it would be easy to work for twenty hours each day. However, people who use time effectively become strategic about investing their time; they ask:

❑   Do I have to do this? Why?
❑   Do I want to do this? What are the benefits?
❑   What 'value' is added by this activity?
❑   What is the easiest way?
❑   Can I use other resources to help?
❑   Can I do something else as well?

The concept implicit in the phrase *investing time* is extremely useful. Regard your time in the way a successful financial investor manages a portfolio of shareholdings. The issues are similar. The investor cannot possess a stake in everything and therefore selects specific holdings, trying to balance the total investment so that the overall output is most beneficial. Similarly, a manager has a finite amount of time and should invest it so that the overall benefits are maximized.

DUALLING

The question 'Can I do something else as well?' was inspired by the successful managers and supervisors who find ways to 'kill two birds with one stone'. We have taken this idea further and have developed a technique that we call dualling. Dualling is the conscious use of blocks of time for more than one purpose. Two simple examples make the point: a train journey can be used to read a technical journal and an after-dinner discussion is an opportunity to test your views and learn from others. Because each block of time becomes an opportunity to accomplish several objectives, you need to be aware of the creative options available. The use of dualling can become a stimulating and productive approach to management and to daily life.

 EFFECTIVE USE OF TIME

Managers who use time effectively share five characteristics:
1. They are thrifty with their time because they perceive it as a valuable resource to be invested wisely. Before making a decision to spend time on a particular activity, the manager considers whether it is likely to be of real value. Activities that bear little fruit are quickly pruned.
2. They develop delegation skills. Delegation is the process of passing tasks to another person. When responsibility, authority and capacity to take initiative are assigned elsewhere, time is made available for new activities.
3. They plan the use of their time. Activities are scheduled, and some form of time plan is prepared so that rational decisions about allocation of time can be made.
4. They use an effective problem-solving approach. When difficulties occur or solutions have to be found, the time-effective manager will adopt efficient processes that lead to a solution of the problem.
5. They are personally efficient. They do not write a paragraph when a sentence will do or take half an hour in a meeting when five minutes will do.

BALANCE

The idea of balance is beguilingly simple: all sides of the person (emotional, physical, intellectual, social and spiritual) should receive nourishment day by day and month by month. This viewpoint was adopted by the ancient Greeks who shaped their lives to fulfil each dimension of human potential. In the Middle Ages the structure of the monastic day was developed so that monks and nuns had a structured life that was balanced and fulfilling.

In the twentieth century the ideas of balance and harmony enjoyed a renaissance with the development of holistic psychology. The same ideas took a new form, expressed in ways that found echoes in New Age thinking.

All this may seem remote from management. Yet the principles of harmony and holistic balance have found their way into organization design. Japanese workers regularly start the day with a physical workout and there is increasing acceptance that the spiritual dimension is relevant to managers. Meaning, connection and environmental responsibility are words current with leaders today.

Each of us must strive to balance our lives. As things change and new forces enter so a new balance must be found. This is an active, responsive process. One simple way to test your own level of balance is to answer these questions:

1. Do you feel fully content, nurtured and fulfilled by your pattern of life?
2. Are you content with your physical energy and fitness? Are you proud of your appearance?
3. Are you content with your intellectual development? Do you feel that this is a rich time for learning in your life?
4. Do you have fulfilling relationships with others? Is your social network satisfying, supportive and enriching?
5. Is your quest to touch and relate to higher forces or deeper meanings fulfilled? Do you have a link with the wider universe which means something to you?

CHARACTERISTICS OF MANAGERS WITH COMPETENT/INCOMPETENT SELF-MANAGEMENT

In summary, managers who are competent at managing themselves tend to show the characteristics listed in the right-hand column shown here. Those who are incompetent at managing themselves tend to show the characteristics listed in the left-hand column as follows:

Self-management incompetence	*Self-management competence*
Neglects own physical health	Maintains good physical health
Works excessive hours	Limits working time
Fails to take vacations	Plans and takes refreshing vacations
Travels inefficiently	Travels intelligently
Withholds expression of feelings	Expresses feelings
Avoids self-insight	Seeks self-insight
Uses time poorly	Uses time well
Is out of touch with own energy	Is in touch with own energy
Neglects meaningful contact with others	Develops meaningful contact with others
Cannot accept failure	Sees failure as inevitable and useful
Has low self-esteem	Has high self-esteem
Seeks approval at all times	Can tolerate disapproval or being disliked
Becomes overstressed	Avoids excessive demands
Accepts impossible challenges	Manages challenges
Often feels weak	Usually feels strong
Takes on excessive loads	Takes on only manageable loads
Leads unbalanced life	Balances personal/work activities

WHEN MANAGERS MOST NEED COMPETENT SELF-MANAGEMENT

Self-management competence is needed most of all by managers who work under pressure, have substantial choice about how they spend their time, make important decisions without reference to others or have conflicting demands made on their time and resources. Self-management competence is also needed when the job requires the manager to make bold public statements or take unpopular stands. Managers particularly need self-management when they must travel and stay away from home a great deal or spend many hours in meeting and entertaining new people. Management jobs of this kind can easily erode leisure time and family life.

BLOCKAGE

2

NEGATIVE PERSONAL VALUES[1]

A young manager, Andrew, went to see an experienced mentor, Martin, for career counselling. The purpose of the session was to help transfer the distillation of Martin's years of experience to the newly graduated Andrew. The following is a segment of their discussion:

Martin: How are things going?

Andrew: Pretty well. Plenty of problems, of course.

Martin: What kind of problems?

Andrew: Well, analysing situations and choosing between options. It's hard to keep abreast of relevant factors. The worst situation is when you are not sure what you're trying to do in the first place.

Martin: I've always found that problems can be divided into two main categories. One category is concerned with finding the best way to achieve a specified goal. The problems in this category I call 'technical problems'. The second category is much trickier – it's concerned with choosing the right or appropriate way to behave. The problem is not how to do it but what has to be done. I call the problems in this category 'value problems' because, in the end, it all depends on what you think is important and worthwhile.

In my experience the value problems present more of a challenge to most people. I think it is part of a manager's job to have a clear stand on such matters. Like it or not, we are all concerned with moral choices.

Andrew: I'm not involved with moral issues. My job is to get things done. They hire me to solve problems and achieve results. It's for politicians and priests to explain why we do things. I am a manager and that means I am supposed to get things done.

Martin: It's true that your job is to get things done. But you are also a kind of gardener and your job is to cultivate a healthy and productive unit. That requires more than slick problem solving on your part. You need to know where you stand in relation to building a community.

---

[1] Some of the material here first appeared in the authors' *Clarifying Organizational Values*, Gower, 1989.

As both managers talked further, it became clearer to Andrew that there was a real distinction between technical problems and value problems. He agreed that, as a developing manager, he needed to determine his own position on values. In order to understand what issues were involved, he decided to seek answers to the following questions:

❏   What are values?
❏   Why are values important?
❏   How can values be clarified or changed?
❏   What values should managers adopt?
❏   How should value dilemmas be worked through?

 ## WHAT ARE VALUES?

Everyone makes choices about what to do and how to do it. You can decide to get up in the morning or stay in bed; to eat like King Henry VIII or a Hindu holy man; to work with total absorption or just do the minimum. The choices made are influenced by our upbringing, the behaviour and views of others and the consequences of our past actions. There are often several alternatives to choose from and each decision depends on what is considered important or right.

Your decisions – what you choose as important or right – greatly influence your life, the way you relate to others and the kind of person you become. Past decisions guide the way you act; they are the expression of your values. Values are choices you make about what is important and worthwhile.

A value is a belief in action. It is a choice about what is good and bad, important or unimportant. Values shape behaviour but values need to be acted upon to be real. Espoused beliefs which are never effected remain aspirations. Values are hard to define yet, like the foundations of a building, they underpin who we are and how we operate. If the foundation is weak the building will collapse. Every individual has a system of values whether that fact is known or not. As it happens, today is New Year's Eve and your authors have decided to spend their holiday writing rather than caring for the homeless, shopping, going to a religious retreat or tunnelling into the vault of a bank. It is our belief that writing is a worthwhile activity (and others are less important) that impelled us to select this way of spending New Year's Eve.

We believe that successful management philosophies are based on fundamentally decent values; otherwise the right to manage is not earned. In periods of rapid change or confusion, people need a rock to stand on. This gives the confidence to enter the unknown and effectively manage change. A strong set of beliefs and values provides the necessary foundation for coping with difficulty.

We believe that managers have to clarify their own values in twelve areas. Each value is associated with 'success'. The twelve areas are:

1. *Power* Managers have the knowledge, authority and position to decide the mission of the enterprise, acquire resources and make decisions. The successful manager understands the inherent power of his/her position and takes charge of the organization's destiny. He/she adopts this value: *managers must manage.*

2. *Elitism* The management task is complex and important. It demands high-quality people to fill management roles. An inadequate manager can wreak havoc – both by sins of commission and by sins of omission. The successful manager understands the importance of recruiting the best possible candidates for management jobs and of continuously developing their competence. He/she adopts this value: *cream belongs at the top.*

3. *Reward* The performance of those who lead an organization is crucial. Managers need to perform consistently and energetically in pursuit of the organization's goals. The successful manager identifies and rewards success. He/she adopts this value: *performance is king.*

4. *Effectiveness* Focusing on the right issues must be a constant concern. Unless effort is well directed, somewhere a smarter management will find ways of taking your market. A successful manager is able to concentrate resources on activities that get results. He/she adopts this value: *do the right thing.*

5. *Efficiency* It has been said that good management involves doing hundreds of little things well. All too often a small error has a disproportionate effect on the quality of the whole. The drive to do everything well gives a sharp edge. The successful manager relentlessly searches for better ways to do things, and constantly builds pride into the job. He/she adopts this value: *do things right.*

6. *Economy* It is a great deal easier to spend money than to make it. Lack of effective cost control is a common cause of business failure and organizational waste. The discipline rendered by the profit-and-loss account endows the wise commercial enterprise with the ultimate measure of success. Every activity costs money; someone, somewhere has to pay. The successful manager understands the importance of facing economic reality. He/she adopts this value: *no free lunches.*

7. *Fairness* One of the greatest compliments paid to a good teacher is that he or she is 'firm but fair'. Managers, by their actions, greatly affect people's lives, both in work and outside. What they do, and what they refuse to do, affects the quality of life of all employees. Using this power with compassion and fairness builds trust and commitment. The successful manager realizes that people's views, perceptions and feelings are important. He/she adopts this value: *who cares wins.*

8. *Teamwork* A well-organized and well-motivated group can achieve more than the sum of the individuals who comprise it. Most people enjoy the company of others and can work well collectively. One person's talents can balance the weaknesses of another. People must feel that they belong. The successful manager derives the benefits of effective teamwork. He/she adopts this value: *pulling together.*

9. *Law and order* Every community develops a framework of laws that regulate conduct. These provide the ground rules of acceptable behaviour. A manager exercises considerable power over the lives of employees and their families, operating as judge and jury, often without right of appeal. The successful manager devises and honourably administers an appropriate system of rules and regulations. He/she adopts this value: *justice must prevail.*

10. *Defence* For many organizations it is a dog-eat-dog world. In every commercial organization, there are talented people planning to increase their business at the expense of the competition. Many non-commercial organizations find themselves under threat from those who provide their funds. The successful manager studies external threats and then formulates a strong defence. He/she adopts this value: *know thine enemy.*

11. *Competitiveness* The capacity to be competitive is the only sure-fire recipe for survival. This is usually recognized at the top level, but it is less likely that the message is understood throughout the rest of the organization. The successful manager takes all necessary steps to be competitive. He/she knows that in the world of commerce, it is the best who survive and the weakest who go to the wall. He/she adopts this value: *survival of the fittest.*

12. *Opportunism* Despite the most careful planning, unexpected opportunities and threats will occur. A manager cannot afford to ignore the unexpected. It is wiser actively to seek out new opportunities than to allow others, more fleet of foot, to grab the best chances. Opportunities have to be seized quickly, even though this may involve risks. The successful manager is a committed opportunist. He/she adopts this value: *who dares wins.*

In summary, the following values encapsulate the characteristics of high-performing organizations today:

- ❑ Managers must manage
- ❑ Cream belongs at the top
- ❑ Performance is king
- ❑ Do the right thing
- ❑ Do things right
- ❑ There are no 'free lunches'
- ❑ Who cares wins
- ❑ Pull together
- ❑ Justice must prevail
- ❑ Know thine enemy
- ❑ Only the fittest survive
- ❑ Who dares wins.

A manager who lacks clear values also lacks a firm foundation for action and may tend to be reactive or go along with the convention of the moment. You must therefore have an answer to each of the questions listed, even though your values may change in the light of experience. Working through the processes of considering the options and clarifying your personal position takes time but the payoff can be increased competence, firmness, decisiveness and stature.

Because values are unseen they may be difficult to grasp. They can be detected only by examining personal reactions and exploring the attitudes that underlie your behaviour. Individuals often feel uncertain and uncomfortable about their values and they are unwilling to be responsible for the consequences of the choices they make. This can be better understood by examining how people clarify their values.

CLARIFYING VALUES

Values have to be known, consistent, practised and honoured. Values oriented to success need to be constantly reinforced. There is no alternative. Leaders with clear values attract others to them, enabling the organization to develop a consensus about what is good or bad and what is important or not important.

Clarifying personal values may be undertaken systematically. It is one of the few topics in management in which inner beliefs are probably more important than external analysis.

A clarified value meets eight conditions, as follows:

1. *Values must be chosen from alternatives*   Only values that have been positively chosen will be firmly held, since the act of choosing strengthens commitment. Managers should adopt a comparative approach and study successful and unsuccessful competitors to discover the values which have been shown to succeed in their own industry.

2. *Values must be consistent with each other*   Values must support each other; values pulling in different directions are destructive. Managers must study the 'package' of values that they live by, and they should check to ensure that they are intellectually and behaviourally consistent.

3. *Values should be limited in number*   Trying to adopt an excessive number of values dissipates effort and confuses. Values are broad, deep and general.

4. *Values should be actionable*   A value that cannot be put into effect becomes a weakness: management should not be committed to an impossibility.

5. *Values should enhance organizational performance*   Values are an 'enabling device'; they are a means of shaping an organization to achieve its performance objectives. Clarifying values forms part of the development of corporate strategy. No statement of corporate strategy is complete unless it defines the wanted values: what is needed from its people, and what is given in return. This means that there must be a logical relationship between the key success factors of an industry and the values adopted by managers.

6. *Values must be attractive and pride-giving*   People should be uplifted by their values. The values advocated by management must touch a deep chord within people at all levels. Values have to be respected. People feel part of a greater whole when they can identify with the organization's goals.

7. *Values should be communicable*   It is what managers do – symbolic communication – that is vital. The actions of managers must reinforce their value statements. A key leadership task is translating values into terms that are meaningful to each individual. Managers should not adopt a value unless it can be demonstrated. This means that the first group to adopt a value must themselves be managers. From time to time managers should collect data from subordinates to see what messages their unconscious behaviour is communicating.

8. *Values should be written down*   The act of writing down values has three benefits: it clarifies the mind, provokes debate, and provides a message which can be communicated.

Clarifying or changing personal values will never be easy. There is much inertia built into us. Habits run deep and are therefore resistant to change. Sustained effort is needed, especially in the beginning.

It will be hard to measure the effort needed to clarify personal values. By definition, there are no objective tests to measure the soundness of a value. Acts of faith are required, as are debate, reflection, experiment and conscience.

Each manager should aim to develop a balanced and progressive management philosophy that is realistic, fair, inspiring and positive. The philosophy will be established by the implementation of each of the twelve values previously described. There are checks and balances built into the theory, which help prevent tyranny or exploitation.

Clarification of values requires answering questions. We have found the following helpful in pinpointing the issues involved in the dilemmas facing managers.

VALUES CHECKLIST

Authority
Should it be respected?
Who should have it?
When should it be questioned?
How should it be questioned?

Gender equality
Should people be treated equally?
Should women have special benefits?
Should gender influence behaviour at work?

Racial equality
Should racial characteristics affect relationships?
How can you exploit, rather than be threatened by, diversity?

Age
Do you value people differently because of their age?
How do your expectations of age affect your behaviour?

Professional standing
How much do you respect expertise?
How far do academic qualifications affect your valuation of a person's worth?

Risk taking
How comfortable are you with taking risks and under what conditions?
Will you take risks that involve the fortunes of others?

Output
How much should be sacrificed for results?
What is satisfactory performance?

Support for others
How much support should be provided for disadvantaged people?
Should people live with the consequences of their actions?
How much support should be provided for sick people?
Is giving emotional support to others part of your job?

Rewards/punishment
Do people respond well to punishment?
What kind of discipline works best?
How far should standards be enforced?
What really motivates people?

Legality
Should the spirit of the law always be upheld?
Should the letter of the law always be upheld?

Win/lose
Do you want to win?
What does winning mean?
Do others have to lose?

Participation
Do you want 'open' management?
How active are you in involving others?
Should power be shared?

Life/work
How much of your energy should go into work?
How important are your family and friends?
How important is your health?

Environment
What is your responsibility to the environment?
What will you do to protect the environment?
What damage to the environment is acceptable?

Enjoyment
Should life be enjoyed?
Should business be fun?
Is creativity important to you?

Openness
How far should you carry being truthful?
Is it helpful to expose your 'weaknesses' to others?

These and many other questions have to be worked through.

Clarifying personal values involves reviewing and reassessing existing values and discovering one's attitudes concerning matters previously ignored. Often this is difficult to accomplish because emotion, apparent irrationality and conflicting interests affect judgements. It takes time to explore the underlying and hazy viewpoints that shape behaviour. The time spent on reflection may be resented as the pressing demands of the present insist on attention. However, without such an investment of effort, the inquiry into 'Who am I?' cannot progress.

The person who proceeds with this exploration of personal values will gain clarity and sincerity – assets for managers whose work requires making difficult decisions and maintaining key relationships with others. The good manager commands the respect of others who recognize that they are in the presence of a person who has worked to identify a personal position. Therefore, the clarification of personal values becomes a tool for increasing a manager's effectiveness in an often stressful and demanding world.

As you go through the process you will learn more about your views and the strength and depth of your feelings. This exposure of your views is part of the process of clarification. Reflection helps in value clarification, but a more expressive approach is usually needed. We favour writing about one's attitudes and values. An easy way to begin is by writing the word ME in the centre of a large sheet of paper and then noting your values as they come to mind. As you see a link between items, draw a line connecting them. By listing your values, you can explore their gaps, overlaps, apparent inconsistencies and areas that are developed richly or poorly. This graphic technique can reveal unexpected aspects of yourself and extend your self-awareness.

People often determine their values and then ignore them in practice. This may be because people express views they feel they 'ought' to hold rather than beliefs to which they are genuinely committed. How often have you made value statements that are more liberal, benign and humanistic than you actually feel? Value clarification is concerned with identifying what is real rather than what is socially appropriate. Your values need to be realistically assessed even if they challenge your concept of how you should behave. After a truthful assessment, it is possible to examine the options thoroughly and bring about a process of change.

One purpose of value clarification is to enable individuals to take full personal responsibility for their values. A value is a viewpoint on which one is prepared to stand firm, advocate, strive for and accomplish. However, it may be easy to observe behaviour that is inconsistent with a person's stated values. An example is the manager who advocates a supportive and sympathetic management style, then proceeds to coerce, control and manipulate subordinates and to diminish the value of their contributions. Because other people usually watch carefully to see how we behave in a crisis, unusually demanding situations can be an excellent source of information, providing feedback concerning where and when our values do not stand up to the pressures of the moment.

New experiences and insights influence individuals and certain of their values undergo change, but not easily. Fundamental change is accomplished only when the old values are found to be inadequate and produce undesirable results. Here, the tool for learning about the effects of your values is open feedback. When you expose your valuation stance you receive the comments and reactions of others. It would be naive to change a basic belief simply because you receive criticism and it would be foolish to retain a belief that has been shown to conflict with experience. If you wish to explore your values, we suggest that you involve yourself in discussions with friends and colleagues, ranging over matters of principle. You can use the Values Checklist on p. 55 to stimulate your inquiry. While attacking and defending the positions of others, remember that the purpose of such discussion is to clarify thinking, not to prove the superiority of your own position.

 ## MANAGERIAL VALUES

Managers do not work in isolation. They are influenced by the prevailing values within the management group, especially the views and personal philosophies of senior managers. As it is necessary to conform to the corporate style to some extent, this can cause problems for the individual manager. The alignment of personal and corporate views can range from support to disagreement, as follows:

1. *Fully supporting the corporate view*   In this ideal position, your energy goes naturally toward promoting the company approach.
2. *Accepting the corporate view*   You understand the company position and have no real difficulty in supporting it.
3. *Living with the corporate view*   Despite definite differences between your own views and those of your company, you can live with the company approach. You may be able to influence the company and make its approach more compatible with your own.

4. *Disagreeing with the corporate view* In this most difficult posi-
    tion, you are expected to support a view that is contrary to your
    personal views. Your options include grudging acceptance, sabo-
    tage, ignoring the corporate view, attempting to influence it,
    or withdrawal.

In conflicts over values, it helps to take active steps to clarify the
corporate viewpoint because the conflicts may arise through mis-
understanding and poor communication.

When a manager is perceived as transgressing the limits of appropriate corporate behaviour, ways will be found to try to 'bring him/her
back into line'. A person may be so at odds with the corporate view
that he/she is punished. This may include sending him/her to the
corporate equivalent of a Siberian salt mine or even ejecting him/her
from the system altogether. Such conflicts help to identify individual
and corporate boundaries and to clarify their differences. Sometimes
making any choice is difficult because open confrontation would result
in punishment, withdrawal would mean a personal crisis and acceptance would diminish strength and vitality. In such a situation there is
a point at which one must take a stand and live by the consequences.

 ## ACTIVE OR PASSIVE MANAGERS

It makes sense for a person to try to become more open and positive
toward life. This is a particular asset for managers who are responsible for energizing others to take initiatives and achieve results. The
basic question is whether to adopt a positive or negative stance
towards the world. An awareness of the distinction has been useful to
many managers.

Those who take an active approach to life are interested in the
experience of achieving and making contact with others. They see
situations as opportunities. They seek realistic but stretching challenges, take prudent risks and are prepared to experiment for their
own growth. They seek feedback and they favour open and non-
exploitative relationships with others. They are open to change
throughout their lives and go through periods of reappraisal and
adaptation. Their experience is not placid because highs and lows are
deeply felt.

Those who take a passive stance are characterized by their lack
of openness and by their restricted development. They find it hard to
be venturesome, tending to become trapped in enduring routines

that offer little satisfaction or self-development. Risks and challenges are evaded or sometimes are taken with scant regard for personal well-being. Relationships with others tend to be superficial or negative, feedback is resisted and communication is uncreative. Passivity may be accompanied by devious or exploitative behaviours that damage relationships.

There is a passive and an active side to each individual and no one is completely in one category. You can decide which part of yourself you wish to support and encourage. Such a decision is fundamental because, if you fail to value and support an active characteristic, then, by default, the opposite characteristic will grow in strength. Typical of the active and passive characteristics to be found in human behaviour are the following:

Active characteristics	*Passive characteristics*
Seeks challenge	Tends to avoid challenge
Uses time and energy as resources	Misuses time and energy
Is in touch with own feelings	Is out of touch with own feelings
Shows concern for others	Lacks responsiveness to others
Seeks to be open and honest	Uses manipulation
Stretches self-development	Avoids experiences that stretch self-development
Has clear personal values	Is unclear about own values
Sets high standards	Accepts low standards
Welcomes feedback	Avoids feedback
Sees things through	Opts out
Tolerates and uses opposing viewpoints	Is intolerant of others' views
Uses conflict constructively	Finds conflict negative
Gives freedom to others	Restricts freedom
Is generally happy about life	Avoids self-insight

The active manager who has clarified his/her values towards those who contribute to organizational success will thrive.

CHARACTERISTICS OF MANAGERS WITH POSITIVE/NEGATIVE VALUES

In the following list, those who demonstrate negative values tend to behave in ways described in the left-hand column while those who demonstrate positive personal values are more aptly described by behaviour described in the right-hand column:

Negative personal values	*Positive personal values*
Fails to question values	Frequently questions values
Ignores evidence that conflicts with values	Changes values in the light of evidence
Does not take value questions seriously	Takes value questions seriously
Is inconsistent	Is consistent
Behaves differently from stated values	Behaves in line with stated values
Does not expose own viewpoints	Exposes own viewpoints for comment
Judges others' viewpoints as wrong	Seeks to understand others' viewpoints
Is unwilling to take firm stands on matters of principle	Takes firm stands on matters of principle
Avoids taking responsibility for own values	Is prepared to take responsibility for own values
Unaware of effects of early life experience on personal values	Has explored early influence on personal values
Adopts a passive stance towards life	Takes an active stance towards life

WHEN MANAGERS MOST NEED POSITIVE PERSONAL VALUES

Positive personal values are needed most by managers who significantly influence policy decisions, who decide matters of principle and who are responsible for advising, counselling and developing others. Some managers frequently make decisions about problems that have no 'right' solution and such decisions must be based on clearly understood and consistent beliefs that the manager is prepared to defend publicly. Managerial jobs that require self-questioning, frequent choices, consistent viewpoints and high personal integrity demand positive personal values.

INFERIOR LEADERSHIP VISION

In the aftermath of the Second World War, Japanese firms attempted to recover from their country's defeat and war-weariness. One small enterprise, a firm called Komatsu, made undistinguished earth-moving equipment (EME) which was neither robust, nor innovative nor inexpensive. In those dark years the chairman formed a strategic intention to 'encircle Caterpillar' and become the leading EME supplier in the world. Step by step progress was made. A quality drive rendered Komatsu equipment as reliable as that of other world-class manufacturers. Vigorous cost analysis meant that Komatsu's cost structure was superior so that prices could be kept low. Full-ranging market research yielded a deep understanding of micro-markets so that special equipment could be designed. Komatsu worked hard to develop new channels of distribution that fitted the changing forces in their industry.

The results? By the 1980s Komatsu was the second largest supplier of EME in the world. Perhaps more importantly Caterpillar was losing money month after month – sometimes as much as $1m a day! By the 1990s Komatsu's advance had lessened but its innovativeness, flexibility and speed of product innovation were legendary.

The management of Komatsu were guided by a management vision which was able to align every aspect of organizational performance. It was this vision that determined strategy, defined the competences needed, made commitment decisions and engaged the imagination of staff at every level.

Managerial visions need to cover all three dimensions: so a manager will have:

❑ Real clarity about what he/she is responsible for.
❑ A vision of service to all stakeholders that exceeds expectations and delights the recipients.
❑ A concept of what needs to be done to improve the organization.

WHAT IS A VISION?

Managerial visions are descriptions of a desired future state. They are tools for grasping intentions and rendering them comprehensible and coherent. Visions can begin with one person but need to be shared by all significant actors in the organization.

A vision is an affirmative statement, an act of true leadership. Yet visioning is not rare. Here are some examples of everyday visioning:

❑   A youth club leader decides to invite unmarried teenage mothers to share their experience so girls and boys can better understand the consequences of their sexual behaviour. The leader has a vision of boys and girls acting responsibly together.

❑   A nursing home owner introduces meditation classes as she realizes that care for the mind is as vital as care for the body. The vision is 'a fulfilling old age'.

❑   A local newspaper director decides to mobilize support for environmental causes and a page a week is devoted to news on this topic. The newspaper's vision is to change the habits in the locality towards care for the environment.

Managerial visions can be of different kinds:

1.   Visions based on logical principles and fundamental beliefs (example 'we will be number one for service quality').

2.   Visions which need to be elaborated and developed, otherwise they are too vague to be implemented (example 'when our company's cleaning division services your washrooms we check service quality on these 83 dimensions').

3.   Visions which need internal consistency. One cannot be committed to programmes which are mutually destructive. Internal coherence, as in a good novel, is a requirement (example 'in order to provide top cleaning services we will invest in state-of-the-art cleaning technologies').

4.   Visions which need to excite support and engage the hearts and minds of all employees. This means that people feel that they can 'sign up' to be part of the process of making the vision become a reality (example 'we will make a computer which is a friend to the intellectual and a stimulus to the non-specialist through ease of use and the avoidance of technospeak').

5.   Visions which need to engender pride in those who are touched by them. Some visions fail because they are too shallow or ignoble. Pride is an uplifting quality which motivates long after

the benefits of material rewards are spent (example 'we will build aircraft fit for our own families to fly in').

 ## INFLUENCING

The magic comes when visions are shared. A leader is a person who engages others in the fulfilment of a vision.

Leadership involves influencing others to achieve a vision. Emotional and personal factors are the keys to influence. Many people are impressed by structured optimism, coherence and that mysterious but real quality, charisma.

The skills and attitudes that generate high influence are not easy to define. They depend partly on the subtle language of gesture and non-verbal communication. However, you can begin to analyse the interrelating elements of influencing by a self-inquiry, answering the following questions:

- ❑ Am I satisfied with my influencing skills?
- ❑ Whom do I influence most?
- ❑ Whom would I like to influence?
- ❑ What is my personal strategy for influencing others?
- ❑ Who influences me?
- ❑ · When do I feel most ineffectual?
- ❑ When do I feel most powerful?

As you answer these questions you are, in effect, counselling yourself. The answers could reveal what is blocking you from exerting influence.

 ## SYSTEMATIC INFLUENCE

The remaining part of this chapter examines those behaviours that lead to high influence and also how individuals, groups and systems can be systematically influenced. We find it useful to consider influence under the following three headings:

1. Influencing others directly
2. Directing others
3. Influencing groups and systems

INFLUENCING OTHERS DIRECTLY

Consider the head waiter at a fashionable restaurant as he welcomes guests and seats them. He knows that some tables are better situated than others and that he cannot offer the best location to everyone. Choices have to be made and some guests will get the best tables, while others will be exiled to the inferior tables next to the lavatories and out of sight of the waiters. In deciding who will sit where, the head waiter is rating people and he may use a mental checklist similar to the following:

Factor	*Question*	*Effect*
Dress and appearance	Are they appropriately dressed? Are their clothes tasteful? Is their appearance imposing? Are their companions impressive?	Appropriate, stylish clothes add impact
Physical stance	How do they hold themselves? Are they relaxed? Are they dignified? Are they physically powerful?	An upright, confident stance suggests personal power
Presentation	Do they know what they want? Are they assertive, rather than aggressive? Are their needs clearly expressed? Are they persistent? Will they stand up for themselves?	Assertiveness skills increase the possibility of getting what you want
Rapport	Are they approachable? Have I rapport with him/her. Do they recognize me as an individual?	Personal contact and rapport aid influence

| Mutual benefit | Am I likely to benefit? Will they cause trouble if mistreated? Will I be acknowledged? | Perceiving benefits increases openness to influence |

The head waiter does not have to go through his checklist systematically because years of practice have enabled him to evaluate situations and make rapid decisions after a few glances and short exchanges. However, we can use the five categories in the checklist to examine personal effectiveness in business, social life and, if rumours are to be believed, even in romance. Try considering each factor individually.

Dress and appearance

Personal appearance and choice of clothes may seem like a monumental irrelevance but we believe they are an indicator of a person's self-image. Much can be read into the subtle nuances of dress. There are many contradictory interpretations, but the following guidelines may be useful. Despite being 'obvious', we often see managers and supervisors who undermine their ability to influence through inappropriate dress and appearance. The essence of dressing well is to be appropriate to the occasion. This means that there are no unbreakable rules. Clothes indicate something about the vitality, the level of risk taking and excitement of the person wearing them. Clothes can serve as a signal that a person is open to experience and wishes to interact creatively with others.

Almost always, cleanliness is also necessary for a high level of influence. People who appear to be scruffy, messy, or simply dirty immediately weaken their impact. On the other hand, excessively fastidious people may appear compulsive – which is also a poor basis for influence.

However trite and simplistic these comments may seem, the fact remains that appearance does affect leadership performance and credibility. Even Lenin, one of the most influential people of the twentieth century, always wore a suit! It is, therefore, useful to consider the impact that your own personal appearance has on others and to ask for honest comment from those friendly enough to offer it.

Physical stance

As psychology comes of age as a science, it rediscovers insights that have been popularly accepted for a long time. Generations of novelists have used descriptions of a character's physical appearance and movements to indicate their mental and emotional state. For example, a person with rigid attitudes often reflects this in a rigid posture and a person who is demoralized adopts a sagging, overburdened appearance.

This connection between the physical and emotional stances of people and the way they hold their body is logical. Years of holding the body in a certain way will lead to uneven development: muscles that are well used develop, while those that are neglected lose their tone.

People who are comfortable and confident signal that they are at ease with themselves and in touch with their own feelings. Watch international leaders on television. See how they maintain attraction and poise even in the most demanding tests of character – played out before an audience of millions. Leaders show a poise and personal strength that means they are not thrown off balance and they continuously create a positive impression without having to sell themselves to do so.

The stance that an individual adopts is a sign of that person's personality, affecting every aspect of life: it liberates or inhibits energy, promotes boldness or meekness and increases the chance of failure or success. Many of the relevant elements of stance – concepts of one's nature and worth – were determined early in life and it is rare that adults examine or strive to change stances they have developed. Fortunately, life-stances are not fixed permanently; they can be explored and redefined. People can choose how to live their lives, and open up alternatives for developing a more upright, energetic and rewarding personal stance toward life.

Presentation

Despite the quality of their message, people who waffle, mumble, or ramble are perceived as less significant than those who present their message clearly and forcefully. As the Dale Carnegie organization has demonstrated, it is quite possible to develop skills of assertive presentation, and thus to increase influence.

We define assertiveness as a quality demonstrated by individuals who know what they feel and what they want, take definite and clear action to express their views, refuse to be side-tracked, and ensure that others know where they stand. Assertion is not the same as aggression. The aggressive person seeks dominance. Aggressiveness involves attempts to intimidate others and violate their rights. The assertive person exercises a right to express a viewpoint and have it fully heard, while respecting the rights of others.

The skills of assertion can be identified and learned, increasing the ability to make a positive impact on others, highly relevant to those in leadership roles. Assertiveness is partly attitude and partly social skills. Attitudes toward self-assertion are learned early in life, often affecting a person in subtle ways.

Assertion brings many benefits, including the following:

❑   Energy is released and this helps you to feel stronger.
❑   You get what you want more often.
❑   Tensions are relaxed, enabling you to release pent-up feelings.
❑   Ideas are communicated with force and vigour.
❑   Decision making is improved because difficult issues are expressed and worked through.
❑   Dominant people lose some of their excessive influence as quieter people gain in expression.

The benefits of assertiveness sound attractive, but there are snags:

❑   The role of the leader is questioned more.
❑   Assertive people state their positions and are therefore more vulnerable at times.
❑   Some people may consider your assertiveness as a nuisance or, at worst, label you a trouble-maker and take action accordingly.
❑   It is also possible that you are wrong!

You can develop skills by observing how other people handle situations which call for assertion. Some succeed, while others fail. By careful observation, it becomes possible to identify some of the characteristics of assertive people. You can extend your repertoire of skills by practising what you have learned. The following guidelines may help:

Build your argument step by step
Ensure that people have the opportunity to understand your arguments in depth.

Say what you need from others
People need to know how they fit in to larger plans.

Communicate in language that others understand
Ensure that you convey messages in ways which make sense to listeners.

Avoid confused emotions
If you are angry, hurt, or emotionally upset, then others are likely to respond to your feelings rather than your message. This can confuse issues and take energy away from your task.

Be simple
People sometimes lose the strength of their messages by excessive complexity or by dealing with several issues at once.

Carry through
Work to resolve questions and concerns which may involve continuing to put your message across until you are satisfied that resolution can be achieved.

Do not 'put yourself down'
>   If something is important to you, ensure that others know where
>   you stand.

Watch out for 'flak'
>   Others, perhaps unconsciously, may try to divert you from
>   your message. It may be because they feel under pressure.
>   Acknowledge their views but return to your point.

Error does not weaken
>   If you make a mistake – as everyone must now and then – avoid
>   feeling inadequate. A sense of inadequacy undermines your
>   position.

People are influenced by those they consider to be 'special' in some
way. There are several ways that 'specialness' can be achieved. For
example the person who is an expert is special, with acknowledged
expertise in a particular discipline. A person can become special by
playing a particular role in an organization and having a position of
authority. A third source is personal contact – specialness is gained
by generating an exceptional rapport with others.

Rapport

Creating rapport is a subtle process with some apparent contra-
dictions. It is necessary to reach out to others without diminishing
personal integrity.

People who show themselves to be approachable earn the goodwill
of others. When contact is made between people, they try to understand each other's viewpoints and are consequently more likely to
value each other's ideas and contributions.

There is, however, a difficulty that should be explored. It is
tempting to *pretend* to be interested in others with the intention of
gaining rapport. Encounters then become based on manipulation
rather than personal contact. Such relationships have an inherent
weakness, as their lack of genuine contact undermines trust. People
often attempt to manipulate each other, so that their exchanges all
have hidden intent. This may suffice for a superficial contact, but if
influence is to go beyond the trivial, genuine relationships must be
built on the basis of trust and honesty.

Mutual benefit

Many relationships are based on an assumption that both parties will
invest their time and energy and, in return, gain some benefit. In this
case there is a contract, similar to the legal sense, between the people

involved. Sometimes the contract may be written down or otherwise explicitly agreed, but it is more frequently implicit.

Rewarding others is often considered to be simply improving their material well-being but there is a range of psychological rewards that are powerful and cost nothing. Berne[1] described the giving of these psychological rewards as 'stroking'. A stroke is a unit of social exchange between people, a sign that one person values the existence of another. Berne pointed out that strokes affect psychological health. They can be positive or negative. A positive stroke helps another person to feel stronger or better; it is an act of support and recognition. A negative stroke diminishes the self-esteem of the other, causing that person to feel smaller or weaker. Those who give positive strokes help others to thrive.

A whole theory of managerial communication and motivation can be developed from this straightforward idea. There are two methods of motivating others. The first method is based on giving positive strokes, thereby reinforcing the other person and encouraging behaviour that is constructive. This form of motivation is accurately called 'positive reinforcement'. The second method is based on negative stroking. The manager seeks out inadequate performance and punishes it, using 'negative reinforcement' to reduce errors and to stimulate better performance. The theory of negative reinforcement works on the principle that people seek to avoid discomfort or disapproval and will behave as directed. The premise is that people can be effectively motivated by fear. We believe that the person who seeks to communicate effectively will choose the first method, positively reinforcing the behaviour of others and developing ways to support them should any difficulties or setbacks arise.

DIRECTING OTHERS

Leadership and command are close companions. When a manager has organizational power more direct influencing techniques can be used. If we examine techniques for directing others, we discover that some are much more likely to be effective than others. Several different approaches can be identified:

Vague directives

> We see managers and supervisors attempting to control others by giving general and unspecific instructions, such as: 'You know you ought to be doing better.' Vague directives stand little chance of producing useful benefits.

---

[1] E. Berne, *What do you say after you say hello?* New York: Grove Press, 1972.

Reasoning

A manager or supervisor may appeal to the logic, sense of self-interest, or loyalty of another person by using such expressions as: 'If we do not get the production out we will lose that big export order.' The reasoning approach can be effective when it is well applied and the other person can see why he/she should change their behaviour. It is only useful, however, when the other person subscribes to the beliefs and values of the manager or the organization as a whole.

Threats

Sometimes we hear such expressions as: 'If you don't increase production to twelve an hour I will play hell.' Threatening operates on the principle that people can be motivated by fear. Fear is a double-edged sword. Resentment can build up and bounce back on the manager. As a tactic, threat always involves a struggle of wills between two people and there has to be a loser.

Pleas

Here the manager or supervisor tries to appeal to the better nature of another person and tries to win sympathy using such phrases as: 'Please get the production out, or my boss will be angry with me.' Again, the plea can work, but only if there is a good relationship between the manager and the subordinate.

Inducement

A manager or supervisor may offer to give an employee a benefit if he or she changes behaviour in a certain way. Typical of this approach is the expression: 'I will see that you have an easy day tomorrow if you complete this order tonight.' Inducement does work in some situations. It is, in a sense, a fair approach, giving an employee unusual benefits in return for unusual efforts. However, if it goes beyond the bounds of fairness, the technique becomes manipulative and ineffectual.

Requests

A manager or supervisor may use the rules of conventional etiquette to ask an employee to undertake a particular task, for example: 'Please increase the rate of production to twelve per hour.' This approach is undramatic but straightforward, and shows respect for the other person.

Explicit objectives

A manager who is concerned with giving clear objectives may use a phrase like the following: 'The objective is to increase output to twelve per hour by Thursday!' Explicit objectives have the advantage of being specific and honest – they demand a response of some kind. When objectives are teamed with success criteria they become even more valuable management tools.

Each of these techniques can work and that is why most managers continue to use them. However, experience shows that some managers are much more effective than others. The following guidelines are offered for those trying to shape the behaviour of others:
1. Be clear and to the point.
2. Approach the person in a way that shows respect.
3. Confront issues, lay them on the table, and work through them.
4. Gain a reputation for being fair in dealings with others.
5. Clarify what needs to be done.
6. Ensure complete understanding and 'sign up'.
7. Agree explicit success measures.

INFLUENCING GROUPS AND SYSTEMS

In conveying management visions managers need to influence groups or wider systems within organizations. For example, a personnel manager may wish to influence the way managers exercise their authority; a financial manager may wish to change procedures relating to budgeting; or a marketing manager may wish to increase awareness of the need for consistent quality.

When developing a strategy for influencing groups, we have found the following guidelines very useful:

Assist self-evaluation
> The greatest force for change is a genuine recognition of its necessity. This means that people should be encouraged to reassess their current situation, see their flaws and inadequacies and want to do something to improve matters. The goal is to deepen and widen awareness of the inadequacies and opportunities in the present position and increase willingness to manage the future.

Be practical – start with small changes and let them grow
> Large-scale programmes of change are often seen as daunting and provoke resistance. Small changes in a consistent direction are more likely to bring success, furthering incremental progress.

Demonstrate by example
> When trying to influence others, demonstrate that you are true to your words. There is no faster way of ruining credibility than behaving in ways that are inconsistent with expressed views.

Reward movements in the right direction
> People tend to behave in ways that bring rewards. Successful influence depends on encouragement, support and rewards.

Agree on goals
> As often as possible, develop processes so that all affected can participate in setting goals for change. Goals that are imposed

without the support of those who must implement them are subverted in a myriad of subtle ways.

Create realistic expectations

Realistic expectations enable people to plan and prepare themselves for setbacks. This helps overcome the inevitable problems that occur in applying a programme of change.

Collect feedback

Assess the impact of your messages and the extent to which change is being implemented. This enables you to understand how people interpret your ideas and views.

Present time-bounded visions

Give a clear concept of what needs to change by actual dates.

CHARACTERISTICS OF MANAGERS WITH EXCELLENT/INFERIOR MANAGEMENT VISION

Managers and supervisors who can develop and share visions have acquired a powerful set of human relations tools. These skills enhance personal effectiveness and can be used to help others. We find that managers and supervisors who have acquired a high level of skill in developing visions tend to display the characteristics listed on the right and those who have low skills display the characteristics listed on the left.

Inferior management vision	*Excellent management vision*
Lacks leadership	Shows leadership
Lacks vision	Has vision
Is present-oriented	Is future-oriented
Cannot describe a vision	Can describe a vision
Sets objectives without vision	Links objectives to vision
Is not assertive	Is assertive
Is not personally influential	Is personally influential
Fails to engage others	Engages others
Fails to communicate vividly	Communicates vividly
Does not build rapport	Builds rapport
Does not manage change towards a vision	Manages change towards a vision

WHEN MANAGERS MOST NEED EXCELLENT MANAGEMENT VISION

All managers have to lead and influence others. As they become more senior and involved in strategy, creating visions becomes even more important.

LOW CREATIVITY

A few years ago, a friend of ours decided that a life of bureaucratic restriction was not for him. He packed a rucksack and went to Israel to join a kibbutz. For two years he shifted irrigation pipes to grow lemons and became passionately involved in the day-to-day organization of the community. On his return, we met to swap experiences over a couple of bottles of wine. He described the management of the kibbutz and told us that during his stay the leaders of the community had been changed and this had immediately resulted in declining productivity, communal unrest and deteriorating concern for the well-being of others.

As the evening wore on, and the wine flowed more freely, our friend expressed his intense disapproval of the new leadership of the kibbutz. He complained that much human potential had been wasted by the new kibbutz leaders, whose unnecessary restrictions had limited the members' contributions. Our friend then said something very interesting: 'It wasn't that the new leadership was particularly bad or incompetent. They were just uninspiring. The life went out of the place. Ideas had been plentiful but they dried up. Energy and excitement somehow vanished. What had been a joy became mundane. It all changed sadly, incredibly and disastrously.' Later he stood up, somewhat unsteadily, and said, 'It seems to me that the greatest feature of leadership is creativity'. With that somewhat enigmatic statement, he closed the conversation and wove his way to bed.

Some managers believe that they personally lack creative capacity and that this ability is very thinly distributed among the population. This view of creativity is, in itself, uncreative. Creativity is expressed by people in all walks of life:

❑ A school teacher finds a new way to convey the idea of photosynthesis to a class of eleven-year-olds.
❑ A railway official finds new ways to decorate the station so that it is pleasing to the eye.
❑ An industrialist finds a simpler way of packaging a product which reduces the bulk by 40 per cent yet continues to protect the product.

❑   A manager on the fourteenth floor of an office building uses stair climbing as her physical fitness routine and meets two objectives at the same time.

Thousands of examples could be given of the various ways in which people express their creativity. It is unfortunate that so many people allow their innovative capacities to wither because they do not recognize their own potential. Creativity is part of the wider process of innovation (defined as 'acquiring great and small ideas and implementing them for profit').

A lack of creative capacity can seriously undermine managerial effectiveness. In this chapter, we present two primary approaches to increasing your personal creative capacity. First, we shall consider what psychological barriers could be blocking it. Second, we shall examine how you can systematically apply creative methods to solving problems. The chapter also presents some ideas on applying creative thinking to work teams and organizations and concludes by considering how creativity can be woven into organizational innovation.

 ## BARRIERS TO PERSONAL CREATIVITY

Once you recognize that you have much more capacity that you imagine, then the next, and main, part of your personal creative development requires you to identify and reduce the inner barriers that are blocking your natural ability.

We have identified seven factors that have blocked or limited our own creativity or that of our friends. Perhaps you could think of some more. Without looking further in the book, take a few moments to answer this question: What barriers prevent me from being creative? Write the answers either in the space given here or on a separate sheet of paper and *be sure to suggest seven* barriers. Then you will be able to compare your ideas with ours and the combined results should be superior to those produced by our working separately.

My barriers to being more creative

1.

2.

3.

4.

5.

6.

7.

Did you fill all seven spaces? If not, you may well be giving up too early. Take due notice of our first barrier, personal laziness, and finish the job!

1.   *Personal laziness*   Creativity demands endurance, time and effort. Giving up prematurely prevents barriers to creative accomplishment from being broken down. Discipline is needed to assign time to creative effort and sometimes boredom has to be endured. Genuine difficulties and apparently insoluble problems often occur with creative tasks but the difficult stages of creativity can be experienced and survived, if you do not succumb to laziness.

2.   *Traditional habits*   All people develop routines of movement, work, expression and thinking, but habits can be enemies of creativity. Traditional habits should be critically examined, and the question 'Why?' is a powerful tool for that task. By going back to first principles, reviewing the processes of thought that seemed logical in the past, you can decide whether they continue to be effective.

3. *Excessive tension* Being creative often involves feelings of uncertainty and confusion. Almost by definition, you do not know the answer before you begin, and this lack of a secure foundation can provoke excessive tension. Some people experience such tension both physically and emotionally, responding as though they were defending themselves against physical danger. Rigid responses and sensations of pressure and stress inhibit the emotional and imaginative leaps of the creative process. People who are tense try to cling to solid realities and in so doing limit their energies.

4. *Muted drive* No significant development occurs without a felt need for change, the fuel of creative endeavour. The need to innovate can be initiated from within or without. For example, recent wars have stimulated fantastic feats in fields as diverse as brain surgery, espionage, photography and journalism. To be creative, people must feel a need to change, recognizing the limitations of old mind-sets and processes and wanting to find better alternatives.

5. *Insufficient opportunity* Some of the most significant innovations in history were conceived by individuals prevented from conducting their lives normally through illness, imprisonment, or even temporary disgrace. For many people, a normal life means filling their days with routines that consume most of their time and energy; their opportunities for innovation are few. For others, their chosen forms of creativity require external resources and support. Without these, it becomes virtually impossible to collect the necessary data, develop ideas or structure experiments. Creative action needs personal assertion so that time, energy, resources and support can be applied.

6. *Over-seriousness* Creative expression often requires a willingness to play with ideas; sometimes solutions lie with bizarre and extraordinary suggestions. This playful receptivity is not compatible with excessive seriousness and an obsession with rationality. The lack of a playful attitude also inhibits communication with others. The excitement of a new idea brings vitality, but over-serious responses can sap ideas of their strength, making it difficult for others to become enthused.

7. *Poor methodology* The lack of appropriate and effective methods of problem solving and decision making inhibits creative effort. Although, by definition, creative work involves novel thinking, it is possible to find ways of structuring such work to increase the probability of success. The creative process can be examined and analysed in the same way as other aspects of management functioning and it is possible to acquire skills and methodologies to assist in this.

ASSESSING YOUR OWN BARRIERS

Each person is blocked by barriers to personal creativity and it is helpful to try to identify and explore these barriers in depth. It also helps to discuss them with others who know you well. Perhaps barriers cannot be completely eradicated, but it is possible to learn how to reduce their negative effects. In striving to become outstanding, a manager should not only be personally creative but also encourage creativity in others.

 ## CREATIVE PROBLEM SOLVING

The techniques for creative problem solving require special skills. Although the process is never a tidy unfolding of mechanical procedures, the key steps in managing creativity can be identified. Creative ideas come from an unknown source so they cannot be manufactured. However, the conditions can be produced that increase the possibility of a breakthrough. Although the disciplines of creativity can be learnt, be prepared to abandon them when the need arises.

It seems that five distinct stages can be identified in creative problem solving. These have much in common with the framework described in Blockage 6, Unstructured Problem Solving and Decision Making, and you will find additional guidelines there. Creative problem solving makes distinctive demands, which are described in the following pages.

STAGE ONE: EXPLORING THE PROBLEM

Problems have to be explored in depth to provide a basis for generating solutions. A superficial understanding will not do. All the dimensions must be understood. There is a common tendency to try to find an answer before the question has been fully understood, which teachers try to counteract by admonishing students to 'Read the question!' They are right to emphasize the need for people to attune themselves carefully to the specific task. The same applies each time you face a new challenge. Not only do you need to have a task objective but you should also understand the task from both an intellectual and an emotional viewpoint. There are three additional benefits to exploring a problem in depth:

❏ The scale of the assignment can be estimated realistically.
❏ The task objectives and criteria of success can be identified.
❏ An appropriate human organization and work method can be planned.

STAGE TWO: GENERATING IDEAS

All forms of creative endeavour require the generation of ideas. An idea can be defined as 'a leap in the dark' so that, almost by definition, it is impossible to say exactly when an idea will occur. Brilliant scientists have conceived spontaneous ideas and solutions to problems while they are dreaming, doodling, or riding on a bus. Each one of us can increase our generation of ideas and ensure that, once they have been produced, ideas are not lost.

Preparing oneself to be receptive requires a measure of self-knowledge. Those who have managed creative individuals know that their habits sometimes become outlandish and unconventional. One research scientist, who had just started working in a large office, announced that he had his most brilliant thoughts only when his massive hairy dog sat beside the desk. His senior manager, the research director, needed creative thinking, but pets were forbidden in the office. In the end, a creative solution was discovered. The scientist chose to work at night, and the presence of his dog was overlooked.

Two techniques that we find most helpful are private and public brainstorming. Most managers know the term but are unfamiliar with the practice. The methods are based on the principle that ideas are best generated and expressed when their evaluation is postponed to a later stage. Brainstorming is thus contrary to the common habit of reacting instantly to suggestions. There are some straightforward rules that help brainstorming to be effective. Briefly stated, the procedures for brainstorming are as follows:

Private brainstorming

❏ Form a group.
❏ Issue each person with ten Post-it notes.
❏ Designate a topic.
❏ Ask each person to brainstorm silently and write each idea on a separate Post-it note.
❏ Insist that each Post-it note is completed.
❏ Gather the ideas into groups.
❏ Evaluate the ideas for utility and innovation.

Public brainstorming

- ❑ Choose a topic or problem.
- ❑ Write down the topic, preferably on a blank flip chart.
- ❑ Establish a definite time for stopping the session.
- ❑ During the brainstorming period write down all ideas, no matter how outlandish or apparently irrelevant, but do not evaluate them.
- ❑ After the session, list the ideas in a logical order, explore and evaluate them.

Brainstorming generates ideas rapidly and the inherent freedom of the technique enables unexpected, imaginative and unconventional ideas to be developed.

STAGE THREE: SCREENING IDEAS FOR APPLICATION

When you find yourself with a surplus of ideas, put them through a rigorous screening. Some may prove to be ineffective, impractical, wasteful, absurd or immoral. However it is wise to avoid discarding suggestions before all their merits have been explored. It is tempting to try to sort out 'the wheat from the chaff' with ruthless and rapid decision making, but this could eliminate subtle ideas that have value. A more useful procedure is to wait longer than seems necessary and see whether any new connections are made. Try to reject ideas on the basis of logic rather than prejudice or emotion. If the reason for abandoning a promising idea is lack of resources, then question the assumptions underlying the decision. Each idea should be reviewed against five criteria:

- ❑ Will it add value to customers (internal or external)?
- ❑ Is it likely to be effective?
- ❑ Can it be made to work?
- ❑ Is it the best choice among options?
- ❑ Do we want to make this idea work?

There is always a risk of failure or partial success, but the risks can usually be systematically assessed. Your objective is to choose an approach that has the highest probability of success. Once an idea has been chosen, it is wise to follow through with boldness and vigour.

STAGE FOUR: PLANNING INNOVATION

An idea is the embryo of innovation and, if the promise is to be fulfilled, the idea must be applied and tested. Implementation has to be planned, or there is a risk of failure.

An example of innovation demonstrates the principles. Consider the case of passengers on long-distance rail journeys. For years they were served coffee in paper cups from travelling buffet cars. These cups conducted heat so efficiently that passengers inevitably burned their fingers. People amused themselves by watching passengers weaving their way back to their seats, grasping scalding cups. Some ingenious passengers adapted by using another cup as an oversleeve. Eventually, some creative person suggested the development of a plastic cup with a built-in sleeve. This was designed, tested, costed and manufactured. Now rail passengers are enjoying their coffee without burned fingers. The idea of a self-sleeved cup was genuinely innovative but, without testing and planning, it would have remained a dream.

In a sense, people are lost when innovating. They need to clarify objectives regularly and reflect on what is happening. This places a special demand on the manager responsible. Many problems are bound to arise, each requiring a solution before the project can proceed. However, if the manager becomes overconcerned with detail, he/she loses a broad perspective on the overall process. The role of coordinating and innovation is similar to that of an orchestral conductor, because the primary responsibility is to ensure that different components and individuals remain in harmony and work toward the overall goal.

Clear, direct communication is needed if the innovation process is to unfold satisfactorily. Individuals must develop a concept or role within the overall scheme and understand how their work relates to that of colleagues. Clearly, individual initiative is valuable, but it must be coordinated within a framework.

STAGE FIVE: FEEDBACK AND REVIEW

The process of innovation is rarely neat and tidy. New factors constantly appear and each new piece of information can influence the development of the process. For this reason, a means of frequently reviewing progress and realigning objectives and plans is needed.

The need for reviewing an operation is illustrated by two workers who were renewing a ceiling. Both were competent craftsman, and they worked together constructively. Tools and materials were moved into the room, which quickly filled with equipment – plaster, nails, steps, tables, hand and electric tools, board and other materials. In the centre of the room sat an industrial vacuum cleaner, with a tube snaking across the floor. Both workers started eagerly, but they spent an increasing proportion of their time looking for misplaced tools and falling over the vacuum tube. The scene became bizarre after a while, as the floor filled with so many items that there was little space to walk.

Although each individual job was tackled systematically, neither worker stood back and reviewed progress. It would have taken a relatively short time to remove the redundant tools, store the materials elsewhere and provide a convenient environment for work. Instead, the two workers extended their working time and experienced a great deal of frustration.

There are few factors more likely to inhibit creativity than ineffective personal organization and muddled priorities. Because the nature of creativity increases uncertainty, ways must be found to review and collect feedback. This reduces the risk that energy will be poured into irrelevant or confused activities. Maintaining a methodical approach – collecting feedback on task performance and accomplishment, reviewing procedures, and adjusting plans and objectives – is a managerial responsibility, and it is severely put to the test when innovation is required.

 ## CREATIVE GROUPS AND ORGANIZATIONS

The history of innovation is marked by significant breakthroughs made by famous people of undoubted genius, for example, Newton's gravitational theory, Einstein's relativity theory, the Wrights' powered flight, Land's instant camera, and so on. We become accustomed to thinking of creativity as a personal and eccentric capacity – a gift that, somehow, particular individuals possess.

However, a deeper examination of progress in innovation shows that much has been achieved by teams, organizations or communities. Creative accomplishments have often been a consequence of the pooled talent of many people. Although certain individuals have been highlighted for their contributions, they could not have achieved the end results alone. A team or organization has nourished the creative output, giving individuals the resources and back-up they needed. The space programmes are excellent examples of organizational innovation, but history is full of similar cases. St Mark's Cathedral in Venice, the computer and the space shuttle are all products of the creative imaginations of many individuals.

A single individual can handle the creative work of a limited project but when the task becomes large and complicated, creative teams have to be formed. Although the ability to interact with computer networks can help an individual to manage complex problems, there comes a point when individual brilliance is not the answer. The limitations of the intellect prevent large-scale projects from being accomplished by a single individual. Enthusiasm, energy, high morale and courage are also needed. The active support of others does much to sustain the individual during the frustrating development and execution of ideas. Almost everyone has talents that can be harnessed to help a team be more innovative, but individual abilities must be recognized and appreciated before they can be put to use. Members of a creative group must therefore develop as a team by learning about one another's skills, knowledge and potential contributions.

A creative team requires a balance of skills. For example, a production team will need people to translate design concepts into operational plans, to match technical and organizational ability, and to combine marketing flair with solid research work. Leadership is crucial to the group's success because the manager will want to build a resourceful and balanced team containing a broad mixture of talents. The creative team should include a spread of relevant technical skills and a range of personality types to give it balance and energy.

The role of the leader of a creative group is so important that it deserves to be explored in depth. There are those who believe that leadership is a permanent and unchanging attribute possessed by a few lucky mortals from birth, but this is far from the truth. Leadership can, at least in part, be learned. Inevitably leadership styles must be adapted to the demands of the situation and the stage of development of the group. A creative team presents special challenges to its manager. The following are the main problems confronting creative teams.

1. *Emerging objectives* Creative groups may lack clear objectives; objectives may change as new ideas emerge; tasks may be imprecise and the utility of their output may only be evaluated after completion of the task. Often it is not possible to set objectives and simply drive towards them – a more flexible approach is required.

2. *Insufficient support* Because organizations are notorious for withdrawing support from creative groups, such a group must communicate, gain acceptance and ensure support over time (especially when results seem elusive).

3. *Uncoordinated activity* When searching for solutions or ideas, individual activity is often difficult to coordinate. As a result, a situation can quickly develop in which all the group members are engaged in unsystematic initiatives. Costs escalate and performance suffers.
4. *Loss of heart* Snags and setbacks can occur as a project proceeds. They can seriously demoralize the participants and lead to a collapse of the group's confidence, initiative and energy.
5. *Communication overload* Creative teams need to communicate extensively. Sharing, brainstorming and discussion clarify issues. However, too much data can overload the system, preventing key topics from being identified. Sometimes 'groupware' – special computing technology for sharing data and ideas – can provide a breakthrough in managing communication.
6. *Inadequate review* As new ideas and data are generated, tasks change in character and scope. Because it is not easy to stay open to change, continuing to work on outdated guidelines can be tempting. This temptation should be counteracted by review and replanning.

The manager responsible for a creative group will want to watch for these potential pitfalls and plan to remedy them should they occur. There are no foolproof answers. The manager will be wise to identify and discuss all problems with the groups concerned. The group members are most likely to give their commitment and support to solutions they have helped to develop. The primary task of the manager is identifying and raising issues of effectiveness, rather than supplying answers.

 PERSONAL CREATIVITY

Some people freeze when they are asked to be creative. The task requires exceeding usual boundaries and operating on a higher level of imagination. The reaction is to strain in an effort to concentrate on pulling the best from themselves. Such inner straining has an opposite effect, because creative capacity can be diminished by strain and undermined by forced imagination.

Some of the clearest insights into the nature of creativity have come from training breakthroughs in the world of sport. Gallwey[1]

[1.] W. T. Gallwey, *The Inner Game of Tennis*, New York: Random House, 1974.

described two aspects of the human personality. The first, known as *self one*, is always judging, commenting, criticizing, and being preoccupied with success and output. The second, known as *self two*, is intuitively capable and much more in rhythm with the flow of life. As soon as a person begins to play tennis (or any other sport), the voice of self one begins to monitor the performance and to interfere with the natural capacity of self two. Thus the dominance of the critical part of the personality can hinder a performance that is within a person's natural capacity.

This powerful idea is applicable to all creative undertakings. Individuals may approach a problem with preconceived expectations, fail to be fully aware of the challenge or the changing factors and try to hurry toward a solution. In essence, they are 'closed' when they should be 'open'. While working on the creative assignment, the person can be sapped of strength by a stream of doubts, criticisms and strain. It is not surprising that true creativity, which is a subtle human attribute, fails to thrive under such a hostile inner psychological regime.

Personal creativity can be enhanced by finding ways of quieting the parts of oneself that promote tension. A search into one's make-up to find personal barriers to creative expression is necessary. Such an inquiry involves looking impartially at one's successes and failures with the intention of identifying the preconditions for creative performance.

Creativity requires continuous learning. For example, as we write a chapter in this book, we are learning more about what we think and we are clarifying our views. Our initial efforts are full of half-formed ideas and imperfect understanding. Several drafts are necessary before we are satisfied that the output is acceptable. These are useful, however, because a period of gestation is needed before something of value is produced. Our best work comes from the ashes of poorer efforts and this is a delight that can be deeply satisfying. However, there is a sting in the tail – in a year's time we shall look at the material and see obvious errors and painful inadequacies. Learning is continuous. There is a positive link between creative endeavour and personal fulfilment, and people regard invention as one of the most enjoyable forms of human activity. Involvement in creativity exploits unexpected inner resources and substantial energy from most people; it gives them vitality and excitement that are missing from humdrum activity. You may want to extend your involvement in creativity as widely as possible, but it does not have to be 'one giant leap for mankind'. Everyday situations are an important source of stimulation.

ORGANIZATIONAL INNOVATION

Organizations used to have a stability which made them feel like permanent features of the community. Shopping centres comprised identical shops year after year and the morning journey to work was so predictable that it was possible to set one's watch by the people lining up at the train station. No more! Almost every industry is undergoing radical change and although there will be periods of stability, such change is inevitable.

Change means that managers must be innovators, capable of generating ideas (big and small) and then managing change procedures to implement new products and processes. Innovation operates at two levels: radical and incremental. Both levels are important although the skills needed are different.

RADICAL INNOVATION

Radical innovation relates to reworking the fundamental assumptions which shape the enterprise. Here are some examples:

❑   A pharmaceutical firm decides to outsource 80 per cent of its R & D work.
❑   A railway moves from being owned by the public to being a commercial business.
❑   A hierarchical firm removes several layers from its structure and empowers each front-line employee.
❑   The firm reorganizes to focus on markets rather than products.
❑   Information is shared electronically rather than by conventional discussion groups.

Radical innovation (sometimes called 'transformation') is always strategic – it reshapes the organization in a fundamental way. In pursuing radical innovation a manager should:

❑   . analyse comprehensively the current strengths and weaknesses of the organization;
❑   compare against best practice;
❑   show willingness to be radical in thought and deed;
❑   be able to create a 'big-picture' vision;
❑   involve and engage others;
❑   design subtle organizational change programmes;

❏   be able to take difficult and, sometimes harsh, decisions;
❏   motivate through times of upheaval.

INCREMENTAL INNOVATION

Incremental innovation (sometimes called 'continuous improvement') is based on a different but complementary philosophy of organizational development. Here the principle is that sustained change is achieved not through 'big-picture' changes but by a myriad of incremental innovations. For example, a musician cannot write a symphony with a concept alone – every note, every harmony has to be developed in detail.

Those who believe in incremental innovation point out that organic change is deep, solid and sustainable. They will tell the story of a fat man who spent his life going to health farms, shedding his excess flab and returning to his normal lifestyle which led, inexorably, to the return of his beer belly and heavy jowls. For ten years the pattern continued until the fat man calculated that he had lost his body weight five times over but was now 10 per cent heavier than he had been a decade before. Then came the radical solution – incremental improvement. Every calorie was counted, every moment of exercise logged, drink banned from Monday to Friday and so on. Each change, no matter how minor, was a step in the right direction. Then our fat man became the Greek God (almost) that he yearned to be.

In pursuing incremental innovation a manager should:

❏   show willingness to believe in the creative power of people;
❏   inculcate problem-solving and opportunity-finding skills in every employee;
❏   reward all creative ideas;
❏   implement every idea with merit;
❏   prize innovation in the workplace;
❏   change from a directing to a coaching management style;
❏   use specialists as supporters in the problem-solving process;
❏   adopt a stance of 'creative discontent' – seeing every situation as capable of improvement.

 ## MANAGING INNOVATION

All organizations which seek to thrive in the twenty-first century must manage the innovation process. This may read like a grand idea but it is a practicality. An example makes the point. One of the authors was giving a breakfast lecture on creativity to a group of managers who were attending a week's course in a seaside hotel. In the corner of the room was a table laden with uneaten food. 'It's like this every day', one of the participants commented sadly. The hotel management failed to ask why so much food was wasted or whether the guests liked the breakfast buffet (which they did not). Innovation was needed. Customer analysis, experiment and detailed attention would provide the data needed to improve the breakfast menu. There was no reason why those course members should not have enjoyed their breakfasts with minimal waste. That is what both the hotel and the guests wanted – yet lack of basic innovation skills meant that it did not happen.

 ## INNOVATION AND RISK

Innovation contains an element of risk but, in a changing world, the failure to innovate is also risky. Risks are inevitable. They may be frightening and people can invest a great deal of energy in trying to minimize risks, sometimes to the point of starving their imagination. The result of management without risk can be low achievement, ponderous decision making and frustration.

Managers can learn much from wise gamblers who know about risks associated with the fortunes of racehorses and the ingenuity of bookmakers. These gamblers do their homework and go to the racetrack fully informed about the history of the horses. They watch carefully to discover any factors that might affect their researched decisions: the condition of the ground, the appearance of the horse, the behaviour of other gamblers. Money will be risked, but the risks are weighed and, when information is lacking, a judgement is made based on experienced intuition. Then the race begins and nothing can be done except to shout encouragement from the stands. It is at this point that the analogy between the gambler and the manager breaks down. Once the race has started, the gambler can do nothing more; when a manager takes a business risk, it is sometimes possible to change course so that chances of success are increased.

CHARACTERISTICS OF MANAGERS WITH HIGH/LOW CREATIVITY

Management creativity has not always been highly prized, but now it has more value than ever before. Managers with high creativity tend to have the characteristics listed here on the right-hand side, and those with low-creativity tend to have the characteristics listed on the left-hand side, as follows:

Low creativity	*High creativity*
Does not value creativity in others	Values creativity in others
Dislikes being uncertain	Is willing to be uncertain
Does not believe in own creativity	Believes in own creative capacity
Has not explored own barriers to creativity	Has explored own barriers to creativity
Tends to give tasks up	Persists with tasks despite difficulties
Prefers traditional approaches	Will break with tradition
Is overstressed	Tries to reduce personal stress
Is content with the status quo	Feels the need for change
Misses opportunities	Takes opportunities
Is over-serious with ideas	Will play with ideas
Likes conventional solutions	Likes novel solutions
Is unsystematic at problem solving	Solves problems systematically
Does not use brainstorming techniques	Uses brainstorming techniques
Has difficulty in managing creative groups	Can manage creative groups
Inhibits expression	Allows free expression
Fails to learn from errors	Tries to learn from error
Discourages innovation	Encourages innovation
Avoids risks	Takes risks

 ## WHEN MANAGERS MOST NEED TO BE CREATIVE

Some management jobs, such as marketing, research, development, artistic and media occupations, demand particularly high creativity.

High creativity is generally needed when existing solutions lack potency or effectiveness, for example, when existing products or services must be critically reviewed and ways found to improve them, or when entirely novel solutions and ideas would reduce costs or add value to customers. Creativity is needed for defining problems; searching for ideas beyond conventional frameworks; for questioning basic assumptions and harnessing technological developments. All management functions gain from a creative approach.

BLOCKAGE

PASSIVE PERSONAL DEVELOPMENT

It was midnight and the cabin lights of BA28 were dimmed. In the executive cabin some passengers slept, others channel-hopped between movies, several computers hummed, other travellers wrote reports. The plane droned onwards from Heathrow to the Far East. One passenger looked into his fifth gin and tonic with the vacant stare of a sick animal. He had been told that this would be his last flight as premature retirement was to be forced upon him.

His boss's words swam around his mind: 'It's not, Harry, that you are not committed or talented. You've been one of the best for years. But frankly, you are slowing down. Look at yourself, you are jaded and tired, you have just done it too many times. There's no excitement left for you. You've acquired a wardrobe of Tee Shirts with the logo been there, done it.'

Harry protested, 'Doesn't experience count? I'm not finished yet. I'm a trouper, a winner.'

His boss said, 'No Harry, we all have a sell-by date and so far as I am concerned, you have passed it. You are still doing the same things as you were ten years ago, saying the same things and telling the same jokes. I need someone in the job who can bring freshness, bounce and vigour. This will be your last trip for the firm.'

Harry unscrewed another plastic bottle of gin and tipped it into his glass. The expression 'past your sell-by date' went around in his mind. He recalled with a wry grin sitting watching *Death of a Salesman* and he cast himself in the play. 'What has gone wrong?' he mused. 'I'm younger than many of the people in this cabin. Why should I be the one who's past his sell-by date?'

Adapting to change has become an important issue for many people today because upheavals in technology, organizations, markets and competences are frequent and profound. Few individuals are in a position to accurately predict their futures and this leaves them with a question: what can I rely on? External forces are unlikely to support managers, so they need to develop their own ways of coping creatively with challenges and demands; they need the capacity to learn and develop throughout life.

People have countless opportunities to develop themselves. In the first twenty years, circumstances structure the individual's development with physical maturing, schooling and a host of new experiences extending both his/her horizons and competences. In adulthood, externally driven development becomes insignificant and personal development becomes the responsibility of the individual.

In this chapter, the relevance of personal development to today's managers and supervisors is examined under the following four headings:

1. Personal development – what is it?
2. Self-insight
3. Openness and flexibility
4. Professional and career development.

 PERSONAL DEVELOPMENT – WHAT IS IT?

Personal development means different things to different people. We believe that developed individuals do the following:

❏ Fulfil a significant part of their potential.
❏ Develop inner balance and integrity of self.
❏ Take responsibility for their own actions and for their own learning.
❏ Meet their personal needs without damaging other people.
❏ Achieve substantial progress in chosen areas of self-expression.
❏ Enjoy and experience life's pleasures extensively.
❏ Live a full social life – both enjoying rights and being responsible.
❏ Show energy and vitality in their daily activities.
❏ Show themselves open to change and new experiences.

The ideas of personal development are relevant to managerial success. Many managers have profited from learning deeply about themselves. The key principles are:

❏ People are responsible for their own learning.
❏ People learn best when they need the new competence.
❏ People gain self-insight from hearing the frank views of others.
❏ Learning is more likely to be effective if it is directly experienced rather than absorbed second-hand.

❏ People need opportunities for personal achievement and creativity throughout their lives.
❏ More choices exist than people generally recognize.
❏ Emotions and feelings are an important part of an individual; we ignore them at our peril.
❏ Relationships with others can often be deepened beyond one's expectations.
❏ People must learn to experience their own individuality.

These principles can be used in day-to-day life. All personal development is firmly based on one idea: every person has unrealized potential. Of course there are some limitations: age, physical characteristics, health, family situation, education and the external environment can present real constraints. However, if you probe your apparent limitations, many of those that seemed absolute turn out to be amenable to change.

COMMON BLOCKAGES TO REALIZING INDIVIDUAL POTENTIAL

Personal development is as much concerned with removing limitations and barriers as with adding new skills or knowledge. Some of the more common factors that block the capacity of people to realize their individual potential follow.

Family influence

In early life, children acquire an understanding of the world about them. Through experience the young child develops an 'appropriate' way of behaving. Although a child tends to imitate the behaviour and attitudes of parents and significant others, there are times when the child reacts against them. These formative attitudes are so fundamental that their effects are rarely questioned and a person can go through adult life playing out a 'programme' established in childhood.

Personal inertia

Sometimes people refuse to believe in the possibility of change and development. Perhaps they try but fail. Dispirited by failure, they ask, 'What is the point?' This attitude can strongly inhibit change because capitulation before making a full commitment undermines chances of success. When the attitude of 'Nothing works out anyway' is adopted, it reinforces later failure. Obstacles can indeed be serious and a person can be overwhelmed through trying to face them. However, if the feeling of disappointment is challenged, it becomes possible to 'bounce back' with renewed effort. All personal development requires overcoming inertia, and this takes energy and persistence.

Lack of support

Personal development often involves building closer links with others. When a person is attempting to change, he/she will probably experience confusion, discomfort and uncertainty. Supportive relationships with others provide encouragement through the inevitable difficulties of change.

Inadequate feedback

We all judge and observe others. Sometimes our evaluations are complimentary but frequently they are critical. Others can see how you react, make choices and deal with problems, but rarely does an observer feel free to express these feelings and perceptions to others and, in many circles, it is considered impolite to do so. It is unfortunate that the information is withheld because it could be used to further an individual's personal development. Experience suggests that people need substantial amounts of direct feedback to provide them with sufficient data to challenge their own self-perception.

Sabotage by others

Each individual is involved in a complex web of social relationships with people who have an investment in that person not changing; they need that individual to continue being the person they know. Any change in yourself can threaten or discomfort those who relate to you. Often, without realizing what is happening, other people will seek to sabotage your efforts to change by ridiculing, by devaluing or even by direct conflict.

Insufficient resources

It is easier for some people to make changes than others. For example, the choices available to a bright twenty-year-old student are many times greater than those available to a sixty-year-old person in poor health. Occasionally a person makes a significant breakthrough in spite of severe limitations and such an achievement is worth more. However, overcoming enormous odds is exceptional and it is wiser for individuals to stretch for the achievable rather than the incredible. Exciting fantasies are enticing but real growth is tested in practical daily happenings and experiences.

It is easy to slip into vague pseudo-mystical jargon when trying to define personal development. For the practical manager or supervisor personal development is a process by which a person becomes more competent at managing situations, building satisfying and open relationships with others, being strong and enjoying the stimulation and vitality of life. Personal development involves struggling with difficulties and taking the risk to be generally more open and truthful.

SELF-INSIGHT

People who undertake personal development can be shocked to discover that there is much more going on beneath the surface than they had ever realized. This is especially true in relation to emotions, both feelings of pleasure and enjoyment as well as their opposites. People often underestimate their own capacities and undervalue their potential contributions.

The first stage in developing self-insight is, perhaps, the most difficult: deciding actively to explore one's own make-up without prejudging the results. This requires a firm commitment, extraordinary resolve and a willingness to confront unpleasant and uncomfortable insights. Each person has a self-image: people seek to present themselves as they wish to be seen and they may be afraid of discovering that they are different or less substantial than they believe. Apprehension undermines personal strength and is often an empty fear. Because individuals are more capable than they know, the initial step in developing self-insight is learning to risk trusting oneself. This approach to learning conflicts with the common belief that mere outer facts have to be learned; we are defining learning as including an inner exploration.

Once you have made an initial commitment to embark on the exploration of personal development, the question arises 'How shall I proceed?' There is much that you can do to help yourself. There are no set formulas and your success will correspond to the depth of your honesty, persistence and interest. If you have the energy to search for help, you will find it. The following are some ideas to start with:

IMPROVING SELF-INSIGHT: HOW TO START

1. *Focused reading* Many books have been written about self-discovery and the psychology of individual development. Some are genuinely inspiring. Discover which book shop stocks this kind of book and then browse. Read books which excite you and try the tasks suggested yourself.

2. *Soliciting feedback from family and friends* Others know an enormous amount about you and their unwillingness to discuss their perceptions may come from shyness or a misguided politeness. Initiate some long conversations about yourself, listen more than you talk, and be careful not to bore your companions!

3. *Undertaking new experiences*   It is easy to fall into a relentless series of repetitive experiences that fail to stimulate. Undertake new experiences simply with the intention of discovering your reactions. Stretch out physically, emotionally, intellectually and socially.

4. *Joining a personal development group*   Many people have been helped by the unique climate and guidance available in a personal development group. Be prepared to be open and only become committed when and if you feel at home with the group. Avoid groups which are part of cults or seek to facilitate insight through intimidation.

5. *Writing*   It is possible to learn much about yourself from freely writing your thoughts and re-reading them later. You may want to burn the result afterwards!

6. *Learning from others*   There are many lectures and discussions on personal development. Sometimes these are well-intentioned humbug, but useful and important thoughts can be stimulated by listening to experienced speakers.

7. *Finding a personal creative expression*   Try to express yourself in some of the creative arts. Drama, music, painting and many other art forms are exceptionally interesting because they require self-awareness. Especially valuable are the martial arts which have been used for generations by those seeking inner discipline.

8. *Seeking physical challenge*   Much can be learned about the self from almost any form of physical challenge. The requirement is that you undertake a physical activity that genuinely stretches your abilities.

9. *Identifying opposites*   You can learn much about yourself by identifying people, situations and activities that you do not like. This contrast clarifies your position and aids self-knowledge.

10. *Reviewing your upbringing*   Your upbringing played an important part in determining how you think and feel. Much self-revelation can be stimulated by meeting people and revisiting places you knew at earlier stages of your life. The most valuable insights can be obtained from simply allowing thoughts and reflections to come to you, rather than attempting to predict what will occur.

EFFECTIVE FEEDBACK

Perhaps the most powerful way you can learn more about yourself is to solicit and consider feedback from others. The word 'feedback' is a term drawn from engineering and applied to human behaviour. Its purpose is to obtain information concerning the effects of behaviour on others. This information provides insight about personal style and effectiveness. Feedback helps an individual decide whether to experiment with new ways of behaving. Managers and supervisors especially need feedback because so much of their effectiveness depends on the way they relate to others. Using feedback can improve group skills and overcome relationship difficulties. Feedback is a powerful tool in personal development but it can be abused. Accordingly, it is important for the giver of feedback to consider how to make comments that are useful and undamaging. With the help of many managers, we have developed the following ground rules for using feedback:

Intended to help

Sometimes managers use feedback with the intention of 'getting even' or disciplining another person. This results in the feedback being received as a punishment and its value in helping the recipient to learn is therefore greatly diminished. Using feedback is intended clearly to help the recipient.

Given with full attention

There are so many preoccupations and tasks in the managerial job that it is often difficult for a manager to devote full attention to another person. Nevertheless, giving feedback is an important and delicate task and it requires undivided attention to the recipient.

Invited by the recipient

Effective feedback is most readily given when actively requested. The person simply says, 'Would you tell me how you felt about me in … situation?' From this invitation, it becomes possible to have an excellent exchange of views. Open feedback contributes to developing and sustaining productive working relationships.

Directly expressed

To be useful, feedback should be specific and deal with particular incidents or identifiable behaviours. The most valuable feedback is direct, open and concrete. Vague, oblique and wary statements are useless and may confuse or frustrate the recipient.

Fully expressed

To be most effective, feedback needs to be fully expressed. Simply touching the surface is insufficient. A full expression of feelings and reactions allows the recipients to consider the real impact of their behaviour.

Uncluttered by evaluation

If you make an observation that contains a judgement, most people will react to the judgement rather than the observation. For this reason, it is better to separate evaluation from description. The most useful feedback encourages the recipients to evaluate themselves rather than accept your views.

Well-timed

The most useful feedback is given when the recipient wants to listen, has time to consider and has the event still fresh in mind. Storing up comments for future use can build up recrimination which inhibits learning and communication.

Readily actionable

Useful feedback allows the recipient to consider whether they are going to try to change the way they operate. Feedback that provides information the recipient cannot use is of little value. The effect may be negative. However, it is useful to suggest alternative ways of behaving so that the person can identify creative options and find new ways to tackle old problems.

Checked and clarified

Whenever possible, feedback should be shared with other people to check whether their perceptions support or conflict with information already received. When different viewpoints are collected and assimilated, differences and similarities can be clarified and the information base becomes broader and more likely to be objective.

Personal growth can be considerably advanced by receiving feedback, and managers can gain by placing themselves in situations that allow feedback to be freely given. Sometimes it is helpful to join a group that uses this technique. In such a group you have an opportunity to experiment and explore your impact on others. Gradually this group experience helps you to identify what kind of person you really are; it also extends your personal boundaries.

An important element in being a developed person is knowing your own feelings and the unique character of your impact on others: self-knowledge requires self-expression. Mistakes will be made and sometimes there will be confusion and disturbance in the feedback process. It does not make sense to be equally open with everyone; therefore, choose those people who have regard for you and experiment by expressing yourself more freely with them. Ensure that you receive feedback while allowing yourself to be more relaxed in your freedom of expression. You will find that the experience brings you more in touch with yourself and, in the long run, enriches your contacts with others.

One common characteristic of all techniques used to heighten self-awareness is that they take time. Many people have found that simple meditation techniques help them to recognize deeper levels within themselves and, with practice, to develop new skills of self-insight.

OPENNESS AND FLEXIBILITY

Managers and supervisors can choose to try to be as open and truthful as possible or to 'play a game' successfully. The choice between being authentic and seeking to play a role is one of the main dilemmas that we confront. Examining the potential advantages and snags of both approaches to human relationships produces the following lists.

The open and authentic approach	*The role-playing approach*
Energetic	Concentrates on skills
High level of conviction	Head rules heart
Expressive	Concentrates on appropriateness
Passionate	Tailors contribution to suit need
Builds trust	Takes a longer-term viewpoint
May be uncontrolled	Can be seen as manipulative
Heart rules head	Self-committed
Can be inconsistent	Avoids emotion
Difficult for others to come to terms with	
Confronts difficult but crucial issues	

We believe that personal development inevitably involves becoming more open and authentic. We do not suggest that total openness is appropriate in every situation. Sometimes it is necessary to curb the expression of one's views. What we advise is to become aware of the extent to which you express your views openly and then question yourself when you withhold your truth.

The starting point for developing openness is to monitor your own expression but try to do this without making judgements. Simply note the occasions when you allow yourself full expression and the occasions when you are less than truthful. You may find that a pattern emerges, revealing that certain people or situations reduce your level of openness. This is food for thought and self-review. Here are some questions you may want to ask yourself:

❑   What common characteristics are there in situations in which I am less open?
❑   Am I afraid of something?

❑   What is it?
❑   What do I have to lose by being more open?
❑   What do I gain through being less open?
❑   What would be the likely effect if I were more open?

Using these questions will enable you to explore your own attitudes concerning openness. Should you decide that it is valuable to develop a more open approach this needs to become a self-development objective.

OPPORTUNITIES FOR OPENNESS

There are no formulas or programmes for openness. Each person needs to seek opportunities for being more open and for exploring the consequences. We asked managers and supervisors to comment on opportunities for openness and their list may suggest some opportunities for you:

In appraisal
> Formal appraisals are sometimes sterile encounters that may do more harm than good. If an appraisal session is openly conducted, it presents an opportunity for an authentic exchange of views and a thorough long-term review.

In counselling
> Counselling is necessary to learn from day-to-day experiences and it continuously develops subordinates. An open approach increases the value of counselling and builds better relationships.

In communicating
> There is a tendency to underestimate the natural intelligence of people. Open communication does much to help people become aware of the realities of their situations and it develops a bond of trust that is invaluable in difficult times.

In talking to seniors
> Those in senior positions frequently find themselves denied straightforward information from subordinates. They find it hard to uncover the truth from those who are attempting to 'pull the wool over their eyes'. Those in senior positions can learn much from hearing the truth.

In problem solving
> Management is concerned with solving problems. The open exploration of causes and possible solutions makes an important contribution to the quality of the problem-solving process.

In labour relations
> Historically, many organizations have played a complex game of union–management relationships. Each side attempts to

outmanoeuvre and outwit the other. Many specialists agree that, in the long run, open and authentic relationships are the best way of establishing cooperative and mutually rewarding relationships between management and employee representatives.

DEVELOPING FLEXIBILITY

Developing the capacity to be open to new experiences and to cope with changed circumstances is vital for a manager. Competence requires continual adaptation to new situations. Several skills are combined in the capacity to be flexible:

- Accurately assessing situations
- Seeing feedback from others as a source of learning
- Listening to others
- Continuously redefining the present
- Not longing for 'the good old days'
- Enjoying challenge
- Admitting error to oneself
- Being aware of the limitations of one's mind-set
- Being prepared to experiment

Flexibility is closely related to openness. When individuals are open, they can be influenced by what is happening around them. They question their established views. The path of personal development lies in the direction of increasing responsiveness rather than resisting challenge.

A STARTING POINT ...

The starting point for personal development is the responsibilities, issues, problems and opportunities that face you. Some people keep their exterior image looking tidy and organized, but there may be a very different story inside. Explore inner doubts and confusions because these greatly affect your behaviour and personal satisfaction.

The individual who chooses an open and flexible management style must learn to be more honest and this is more difficult than it sounds. It is tempting to be devious, perhaps with the best intentions. When people experience something they do not like, their usual response is to want to remedy the situation. If there is no solution available, they may evade facing the problem. With the development of openness and flexibility, it becomes possible to explore some of these unexpressed aspects of the self with the intention of simply finding out what is there. One manager put it this way, 'I have found out that the truth, warts and all, is more important than being comfortable'.

Openness and flexibility are key features of personal growth and their pursuit is the primary vehicle for development. Because of the inevitable difficulties and confusions along the way, close human contact and the support of others are needed.

 ## PROFESSIONAL AND CAREER DEVELOPMENT

In addition to having a job, a manager or supervisor is a member of a professional group. Although some professionals, such as solicitors and physicians, may have closer professional ties, individual managers should explore the relationships between themselves and other managers in different organizations and countries. This can be accomplished through participation in professional groups. The advantages of such participation are that:

- ❏ it broadens your approach,
- ❏ it helps to identify the responsibilities of professional conduct;
- ❏ it builds confidence; and
- ❏ it increases your career options.

Professional development can be pursued in a number of ways and each option has relevance. As you consider the following list of options, ask yourself how many of these activities you have undertaken in during the past year:

- ❏ Taking short courses
- ❏ Attending classes
- ❏ Involvement with a professional body
- ❏ Visiting other firms
- ❏ Reading management and professional books
- ❏ Taking correspondence courses
- ❏ Receiving counselling
- ❏ Reading journals
- ❏ Participating in seminars and debates
- ❏ Trying new management techniques.

STAGES OF CAREER DEVELOPMENT

One aspect of professional development that is frequently overlooked is the way development needs to change with maturity and over time. Careers are now less predictable than at any time in the past 200 years. However, there are some common themes. If a typical career is followed it is possible to identify a pattern.

After foundation education has been completed, a young person joins an organization. In the first few months many unknowns are faced and potential blunders can be made. The main issue that concerns the new person is getting involved and coming to terms with the organization. This phase can be compared to learning a new game: there are rules to be understood and options to be chosen. It is a time of rapid adaptation.

In early years of working, the individual needs to find a place in the world of work and the main issue is 'making a mark'. It may be that conventions are challenged and a bold, almost cocky, stance is taken by the individual. This is the phase of fighting and seeking recognition.

With experience and, perhaps, the demands of a new family, a new phase of consolidation is entered. Personal recognition is no longer a need but the career developer must expand individual competence and become recognized as a sound contributor. Values are rethought and the significance of work is reassessed. People who are in their period of consolidation begin to define achievement in different terms.

Somewhat later, many managers experience a period of upheaval and deep inner reflection when they begin to take themselves more seriously. They question the meaning of their jobs, wondering whether to devote their vitality to endeavours that they had not considered previously. Our term for this phase is re-evaluation and when it is successfully experienced the results add depth and wisdom to the individual manager. Sometimes an external change (for example, a job loss) will throw the person into unexpected re-evaluation.

Still later, the highly experienced manager focuses on the development of others, becoming concerned with the well-being of the organization and the effectiveness of younger people. This is a period of statesmanship, and compassionate interest is shown in the development of others rather than oneself.

Of course, each life history is different and so there is no established pattern but career development stages can be distinguished. We know that many people experience an important and turbulent period of stress and upheaval at each transition.

Five key stages of a typical career development are shown in Figure 2.

During a managerial career there will be many occasions when jobs will change. It is important that new jobs conform as much as

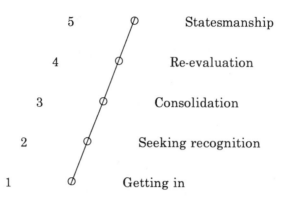

Figure 2 Stages of a typical career development

possible to the personal needs of the individual at that time. A job that fails to help you accomplish your potential will tend to weaken you, no matter how powerful the position.

MANAGING PERSONAL DEVELOPMENT

This section happens to be written on a Sunday morning and the newspaper has just arrived. After the usual news items on war, death, mayhem and corruption there is a five-page supplement on 'Getting Fit and Staying Fit'. Of course, there are the usual diagrams of people with their knees touching their ears but a strong underlying theme of self-management runs through each section – from healthy eating to healthy sex.

The principle is straightforward but powerful: managing personal development requires exactly the same skills as managing any other objective. Consider a police sergeant who is given the objective of reviewing the police methods currently being used to protect vulnerable elderly people. The sergeant will probably:

❑   Clarify the objective
❑   Agree success measures
❑   Develop an information-gathering plan
❑   Break big tasks into small assignments
❑   Allocate time, responsibility and resources
❑   Monitor progress against explicit milestones.

These fundamental skills of management are infrequently, in our experience, used by people to manage their own development. How many people do you know who have a personal development plan *and* keep to it?

The individual manager needs to build competences which remedy weaknesses in today's performance and prepare for future development.[1] Competence is not a simple concept. It consists of five components:

1. *Skill*: being able to perform, in the correct sequence, difficult or complex techniques.
2. *Knowledge*: having relevant data, helpfully organized, and being able to use an appropriate body of knowledge.
3. *Attitude*: constructive emotional stance and willingness to perform to a high standard.
4. *Self-concept*: confidence in one's ability to achieve.
5. *Perceptual sharpness*: being able to pay attention to things that really matter in doing a good job.

All five components interact, although one is sometimes pre-eminent. Knowledge is needed for skill, which guides perception, which shapes attitude, and so on. Competences are bridges: they enable people to cross to where they want to be. Imagine a spider's web: thinking, feeling and performing all support each other to provide a competence.

Competences which must be acquired throughout a career vary according to gender, occupation, social class and social mobility. For example, women may transfer from work into family life and then back into work. This can require a great deal of new learning.

We must continue to learn and develop throughout our lives. Transitions occur perhaps once a decade and cannot be prevented. Although people may ignore or attempt to evade the next transition, the logic of biological ageing and contingent change of career focus is inexorable. Sometimes unexpected transitions, like illness or redundancy, are imposed without warning and new competences are suddenly required to cope with a previously unknown situation. Those who say that they have been successful in managing unexpected transitions report that they:

❑   had enough money;
❑   undertook a radical review;
❑   discussed their situation;
❑   received counselling;
❑   enjoyed warm support;
❑   carefully identified what new competences were needed;
❑   took initiatives to get training;
❑   were prepared to be bold.

---

[1] Some of the material in this section is drawn from Dave Francis, *Managing Your Own Career*, HarperCollins, 1994.

Lack of recognition of your potential is a primary blockage. Reflect on how you operate shortly after you return from your vacation. Most people experience a sense of relaxation, greater enjoyment, more energy and greatly increased capacity to accomplish things. This state would be a tremendous asset if it were with us more often. However, people become jaded and tattered by the innumerable demands that fill much of their daily experience. It is when they recognize the lack of quality in their lives and decide to live more efficiently that personal development can begin. Without this recognition they do not have the required openness and energy.

CHARACTERISTICS OF MANAGERS WITH PASSIVE/ACTIVE PERSONAL DEVELOPMENT

Personal growth is important for managers because their jobs always make significant demands on their wisdom, judgement, time and personal strength. A weak or immature manager is a consistent headache to subordinates, colleagues and supervisors. Managers who are concerned with actively advancing their own development tend to show the characteristics listed here in the right-hand column: the left-hand column describes the manager whose personal growth is passive.

Passive personal development	*Active personal development*
Evades responsibility for learning	Takes responsibility for learning
Fails to explore self	Wants to explore self
Fails to set aside self-development time	Sets aside time for self-development
Evades challenges	Welcomes challenges
Avoids feedback	Solicits feedback
Ignores self-reflection	Sets aside time to reflect
Inhibits feelings	Explores own feelings
Fails to audit self	Assesses own skills
Limits stimulation	Plans to be stimulated
Is unaware of own potential	Believes in own potential
Is unaware of influences on self	Understands influences on self
Ignores professional development	Manages professional development
Avoids career development	Responds to career changes

WHEN MANAGERS MOST NEED PERSONAL DEVELOPMENT

One of the intriguing aspects of personal development is that the task is never completed. No one wins the final accolade as being a fully developed and mature person. Self-development is a continuing effort rather than an objective to be achieved.

Most management jobs require a high level of personal development but, as the degree of change increases, so does the need to adopt a creative and flexible stance. Managers need to maintain their effectiveness despite the pressures. Managerial jobs that involve substantial change require an above-average capacity for personal development. Such jobs may involve technological changes, new markets, revised organizations, or novel challenges. Personal development is also necessary for those who expect to move to more demanding jobs or when they are in transition between important stages in their career. Whenever a manager needs to become more receptive, energetic, creative or resourceful he/she needs a high level of personal development.

BLOCKAGE

6

UNSTRUCTURED PROBLEM SOLVING AND DECISION MAKING

Snow was forecast for all the cities in the north-east of the USA. From Washington to Chicago a blizzard was adding snow to the runways at 1 inch per hour and the storm was moving east. Soon New York, Philadelphia and Boston would be snow-bound. Maintenance crews at each airport were all ready with their snow-ploughs and blowers but the equipment couldn't keep pace. Ice encrusted aircraft wings and passengers badgered ground staff for information.

Each airline in the region set up an emergency team to try to minimize cost and disruption. Computer simulations played with the options, asking such 'What if' questions as, 'Is it better to cancel flight 182 with 20 people from Washington to Detroit and have a plane in the wrong location or cancel flight 141 with 107 people from Washington to Denver and have a plane in the right location?'

Complex judgements concerning resources, inconvenience to passengers, risk levels, system recovery time and costs/benefits had to be taken by weary controllers in their emergency teams. Dependent on their decisions millions of dollars would be squandered or saved. One team recalled that a similar snow emergency had cost United $50m a few years before.

The airlines flying to cities in the north-east of the USA experienced difficulties that day. To be more precise they had a 'big' problem (the closing of airport runways) and a multitude of 'smaller' but consequential problems (such as running out of coffee in Boston terminal and a freight plane filled with live chickens which were freezing to death at Newark). Since several alternative choices were available problem solving needed to flow into decision making in one seamless process.

The term 'problem' is too vague for us to use without further analysis. In everyday language a 'problem' can be many things, from an unexpected happening (the car breaks down on the way to a wedding) to a difficulty in planning ('I have a problem because my son won't take his career seriously').

We divide 'problems' into four categories:

1. *Mysteries – negative deviations from the expected* Something important goes wrong and you don't know why. 'The dog food is

coming out of the manufacturing plant bright green and we don't know the cause.'

2. *Puzzles – something is wrong but you can't find the solution*
There is a 'right' answer but you do not know what it is. 'One of the compounds inhibits the growth of the AIDS virus but the computer has lost the records.'

3. *Dilemmas – there are several choices but it is difficult to know what is best* A dilemma exists only where there are several things that could be done, each with merits and demerits. 'We could wait till the storm lifts or carry the passengers by bus.'

4. *Difficulties – the objective is clear but how to achieve it is not* Difficulties are 'problems of implementation'. What needs to be done may be perfectly apparent but the process uncertain. 'We have two cats that spit and fight all the time. How can we make them tolerate each other?'

Sometimes it helps to think about the type of problem before you try to solve it. Why? Because the most effective methodology varies according to the type of problem. This is shown in Table 1.

Identifying and resolving problems is a continuous function for human beings but too few people receive any help in learning how to tackle problem solving in a skilful and effective manner. Because the managerial job is primarily concerned with solving problems, a mature competence in this area is a key feature of managerial performance.

Problem solving is never easy, but this chapter examines three ways of developing the needed skills:

1. Using a structured approach to problem solving
2. Linking problem solving and decision making
3. Using people and resources to assist in problem solving.

Table 1 Types of problem and effective methodologies

Type of problem	Effective methodologies
Mysteries	Collecting data, structuring data, exploring variations, cause–effect analysis, problem definition.
Puzzles	Collecting data, developing hypotheses, experimenting, removing disproven hypotheses, validating.
Dilemmas	Determining choices, assessing strengths and weaknesses, identifying group decision-making stakeholders, risk analysis.
Difficulties	Identifying helping and hindering forces, building support, isolating difficulties, project management, resource mobilization, tactical management skills.

Each of these methods links together to form an effective problem-solving approach but each also stands in its own right and can be examined from several points of view. We have found that an intellectual appreciation of the techniques is insufficient; it is also necessary to experience the ideas in operation and test them in practice.

A STRUCTURED APPROACH TO PROBLEM SOLVING

It is strange, but true, that any procedure for problem solving becomes less useful if applied rigidly. Therefore, we encourage you to apply the following guidelines flexibly and be prepared to adapt your approach to the particular problem you face. It is possible to work methodically through problems; steps in problem solving are identifiable. If you fail to be effective in problem solving, then is it probable that one or more of the following stages has been inadequately handled. The model that we prefer comprises eight steps.[1]

STEP ONE: TUNING IN

Assess, understand and categorize the problem, discovering what specific challenges it offers. If the problem relates to a group, the team members need to understand the nature of the problem and decide how they are going to organize themselves to work together effectively.

STEP TWO: OBJECTIVE SETTING

An objective is a statement of what an individual or a group intends to achieve. The objective may be clearly understood and accepted or seem hazy or excessively general. An objective should be stated clearly and specifically and it should be understood by all concerned. An objective can be redefined or adapted in the light of experience, and there may be several objectives for a particular task. General or broad objectives are made more specific by asking 'How?'

---

[1] For more detail see Dave Francis, *Effective Problem Solving*, Routledge, 1991.

STEP THREE: SUCCESS MEASURES

Find out how to measure whether your endeavours have been success-ful. Sometimes the statement of your objective can include criteria for judging your performance. If not, you will need to search for ways to assess your performance objectively. Asking two questions can help with the search:

❑   What criteria will allow us to determine 'success'?
❑   How do we measure 'success'?

When the criteria of success have been established, group members will understand clearly the end performance that is required. Hence, just enough energy can be expended to accomplish the task and make the best use of time.

STEP FOUR: INFORMATION COLLECTION

Before a solution to a problem can be found, the problem should be understood in depth. People who are involved with a problem may possess facts, opinions, ideas or prejudices about it. Because the human brain is unable to manipulate large amounts of information, skilful techniques of data collection and display help clarify the problem. New information may be sought, either from within the group or by research. Once information has been collected, alternative courses of action can be identified. These alternatives should be clearly stated so that their strengths and weaknesses can be assessed.

STEP FIVE: DECISION MAKING

Choices are articulated in the information-collection step and now must be assessed and evaluated and a coherent decision made. This step begins with the process of deciding what criteria will be used to evaluate each of the alternative options. The development and weigh-ing of clear criteria is a crucial element in the decision-making process. Then each of the options must be tested without prejudice. Once an option appears to be the best choice it must be examined for potential snags, disadvantages and vulnerabilities before a commit-ment decision is made. The final process of this step is to engage all those whose energy is necessary to effect the decision.

STEP SIX: PLANNING

Planning concerns the acquisition and mobilization of resources to carry out tasks. In its basic form, planning is the process of directing, controlling, coordinating, scheduling and motivating people and other resources to achieve specified objectives. However, planning often goes beyond this narrow definition to include: deciding what competences are needed, acquiring and developing competences and managing the process of continuous adaptation to new circumstances. Planning is never a sterile systems-driven activity as there are constant problems and decisions to be resolved.

STEP SEVEN: ACTION

At this step, the task is undertaken. When objectives and the criteria for success are clear all those concerned know what they are trying to achieve and they can intelligently amend their plans as circumstances dictate. Effective action requires will-power, practice and commitment. The quality of achievement depends largely on the quality of preparation (with a little bit of luck).

STEP EIGHT: REVIEW TO IMPROVE

People learn from seeing the results of actions, from assessing their successes and from trying to identify the causes of failure. Avoid becoming dispirited or pessimistic when reviewing your failures. Without feedback, there is little chance of changing and developing – people simply repeat the same patterns. The adage 'practice makes perfect' would be more accurate if it were 'practice makes permanent'. Because the purpose of review is to gain information and energy to improve later performance, finish reviewing with a statement of guidelines for future activity.

 PROBLEM SOLVING IN GROUPS

This eight-step approach to structured problem solving is a flexible tool. At any stage you can go back a few steps and adapt the pattern to suit both your own work methods and the specific task in hand. It takes time to learn to use it, so be prepared for a period of learning before you master the method.

The approach gives groups a common language with which to communicate. Review your normal business meetings and see whether a more systematic approach would be helpful. We have found that recording, preferably with video, is an excellent way to examine meetings and planning sessions. But this needs the free cooperation of all participants. Video feedback is a powerful way of confronting what happens in a group.[1] It allows individuals to see themselves with an objectivity that is hard to achieve in any other way. The video medium is direct and enables painstaking analysis to be undertaken. Feedback can be given between individuals and difficulties of interpersonal contact can be identified and worked on openly. Because the video review provides a 'temperature check' on team effectiveness, it can be periodically introduced into routine meetings so that progress can be evaluated. In this way, the eighth problem-solving step, 'Review to Improve', can be introduced into practical business life. Managers and supervisors who can use actual incidents as positive learning experiences have done much to increase their personal effectiveness.

 ## LINKING PROBLEM SOLVING AND DECISION MAKING

Problems vary. In the course of a working week a manager may be asked to:

❑   Make recommendations following a feasibility study (a dilemma)
❑   Chair a meeting with people who have a personality conflict (a difficulty)
❑   Persuade a customer to amend an order (a difficulty)
❑   Cope with an unexpected trade union dispute (a mystery)
❑   Decide how to reduce personal stress (a puzzle).

These problems may include information collection, idea generation, complex planning, interpersonal problem solving, emotional issues, influencing others, self-management, conflict handling and plenty of decision making.

[1.] See Dave Francis, 'Using a video system in human relations training' in J. E. Jones and J. W. Pfeiffer (eds), *The 1979 Annual Handbook for Group Facilitators*, San Diego, CA: University Associates, 1979.

DECISION MAKING

Every problem-solving task requires an element of decision making but not every decision-making task involves problem solving. We have found it helpful to categorize four levels of decision making, each of which requires distinctive management skills. As you read the definitions, consider the particular requirements of your job and the demands the job makes on your ability.

LEVEL ONE: ROUTINE DECISIONS

These decisions are matters of procedure and routine. Here, the manager is behaving in a logical programmed way, almost like a computer, identifying situations and reacting in a predictable manner. The manager's function is to sense and define situations, then take the responsibility for initiating action. Inadequate performance results when a manager is insensitive, improperly perceives signs, behaves illogically, makes illogical deductions, or is indecisive and fails to act effectively. The manager who correctly perceives, accurately deduces and incisively acts is fulfilling all that is expected. Creativity is not appreciated at this level because procedures are all prescribed.

LEVEL TWO: EMPOWERED DECISIONS

These decisions involve an element of initiative and discretion but within defined limits. Here the manager assesses the merits of a range of solutions and tries to find the best fit between established policy and alternative actions. Effectiveness depends on the manager's capacity to choose a course of action that has the highest probability of meeting corporate values and policies as well as being acceptable, economic and effective.

LEVEL THREE: INNOVATIVE DECISIONS

These decisions involve new challenges because the manager has to generate a creative solution that is, in some respects, genuinely innovative. Usually this requires a blend of tested answers and some new ideas. The manager's effectiveness depends on individual initiative and the capacity to make a creative leap. Such decisions provide answers to problems that may have arisen before but not in this particular form. The manager is finding a novel solution to a known problem.

LEVEL FOUR: TRANSFORMATIONAL DECISIONS

These decisions are the most complex and demanding faced by a manager. They require a revolutionary innovation to achieve a satisfactory solution. Often the need or opportunity is one that is initially poorly understood and solutions contain totally novel concepts and techniques. The manager must find ways to deal with unexpected and unpredictable problems, and the solutions often involve developing new frameworks of thinking. The most advanced and demanding transformations may even require the development of a new branch of science or technology.

Each of these levels of decision making makes different demands on managerial competence. The following examples make this clearer.

Consider the branch manager in charge of a small shoe shop whose work is almost entirely routine. The head office has established procedures dealing with almost all eventualities, including customer complaints, staff problems, display, ordering and documentation. The manager's task consists of thoroughly and humanely operating within the company's guidelines. When something occurs that is not within the prescribed procedures, it is dealt with only after reference to a senior manager. Although predominantly performing routine work, this manager does make important decisions and a painstaking and responsible approach is needed for the shop to be successful. Using categories of decision-making ideas, this branch manager is working at Level One, making decisions that are generally routine.

A factory manager in charge of a production department operates in a relatively open environment and has to make choices among a number of alternative solutions. This may involve production control, materials handling, personnel replacement, industrial relations and a wide range of other topics. Moreover, the manager is responsible for evolving a healthy, effective and adaptable system. There are many problems in the production department, almost all of which have been experienced somewhere before. The range of available solutions is broad and the manager's task is to select the course of action most likely to succeed. In addition to making a rational analysis of a problem, the manager has a 'feel' for the situation and uses it to determine an appropriate course of action. The situation is complex, with hard-to-define factors interfering, so action inevitably involves an element of personal judgement. It often proves possible to make the chosen answer succeed, if it is pursued with vigour and allocated sufficient resources. The production manager's activities are largely concerned with the selection of appropriate strategies, a characteristic of Level Two decisions, which are empowered.

In another part of the organization is the marketing department. Its task involves creating new solutions for reasonably well-understood problems. Innovative ideas are required from the marketing staff, whether the task is finding a new advertising approach or developing an incentive scheme to revitalize a flagging sales effort. To provide a comprehensive foundation for decision making, problems need to be clarified and simplified and data must be systematically collected. The characteristic of an outstanding marketing manager is the capacity to choose and promote sound strategies that offer genuine novelty and, at the same time, make sound business sense. Primarily concerned with creative adaptation, the marketing manager makes Level Three decisions. These decisions are termed innovative.

Open and poorly understood challenges make special demands on a manager. An appropriate example would be the head of a research centre whose task is to make something distinctive and new. Such an assignment could be a fission reactor, an artificial diamond, or a new energy system. The manager usually begins with a problem that is insufficiently defined and has no known solution. He/she must mobilize resources and assemble an organization that is capable of being genuinely creative. Sometimes new technical languages, concepts, tools, technologies or facilities must be introduced. This means that a large proportion of the significant responsibilities of the manager are genuinely novel and therefore the manager makes Level Four decisions, described as transformational.

In many organizations, there is a direct link between seniority and level of decision making. At the most basic level, the manager needs to take initiatives but these can be reliably predicted. Hence, the junior manager is usually concerned with keeping subordinates' vitality and interest alive, while maintaining performance standards. Higher levels of decision making contain real challenges and involve more senior managers in managing innovation, mobilizing resources and taking risks.

 ## FOUR LEVELS OF DECISION MAKING

The following checklist links the four levels of decision making with the key skills demanded of the manager concerned. Managers working at higher levels of decision making also require lower-level skills. For example, a manager working at Level Three (innovative) decisions requires not only the skills of that level but also those of Level One and Level Two.

Experience demonstrates that it is as inappropriate for a manager to be overdeveloped as underdeveloped. A Level One job needs management skills appropriate to the task. A manager who possesses the skills to manage open, creative, or strategic problems can feel frustrated when there is no outlet for those skills. With his/her potential blocked, the manager may undervalue current tasks, feel unfulfilled and resent a system that seems restrictive.

Managers learn by comparison and experience with accomplished practitioners and by reviewing their own experience, gaining new insights, overcoming challenges and accomplishing tasks. Movement to a higher level of decision making only occurs when the manager becomes actively involved in handling higher-level problems.

Decision type	*Key skills*
Level One: Routine	Procedural discipline
	Sound evaluation
	Humane leadership
	Limited discretion
Level Two: Empowered	Identifies needs
	Generates alternatives
	Understands policies
	Will take empowered decisions
Level Three: Innovative	Identifies opportunities
	Generates creative ideas
	Incremental improvement
	Risk analysis
Level Four: Transformational	New paradigms
	Redefinition
	Radical change
	Transformational leadership

 ## USING PEOPLE AND RESOURCES TO SOLVE PROBLEMS

Managers often need to work with others to find solutions to problems and this may happen in several different ways:

- ❑ Task forces are established
- ❑ Mini-workshops are conducted
- ❑ People work together on day-to-day problems
- ❑ Colleagues counsel each other
- ❑ Team meetings act as problem-solving groups
- ❑ Project groups act as 'tiger teams'
- ❑ Computers link individuals around topics
- ❑ Outside resources are called in.

Problem-solving meetings that encourage diverse viewpoints and technically reliable contributions can assist in defining problems and in finding their solutions. Such problem-solving sessions can be made more productive by following these guidelines:

1. *Clarify who 'owns' problems* People often try to evade responsibility for messy or intractable problems. Because such evasion seriously limits the possibility of finding solutions, be specific about who has the responsibility for solving problems.

2. *Appoint a coordinator for group sessions* A coordinator is needed for every problem-solving group. Newly formed groups are not used to working together and may have problems of conflicting loyalties or poor personal relations. Initially the coordinating role requires the development of appropriate procedures that solve problems and make good use of time. Before a problem-solving group can be fully effective, each of the following areas need to be developed:

    (a) Clarifying the contribution of group members: ensuring that the members' specialized skills are identified and understood.

    (b) Structuring the group: taking initiatives to organize the group in ways that are suitable to the task. This involves working through the eight-step approach to structured problem-solving described earlier in this chapter.

    (c) Clarifying contributions: checking on whether contributions are understood and ensuring that any areas of uncertainty are clarified.

    (d) Asking for ideas/reactions: encouraging people to express their views, suggestions and reactions, especially people who appear withdrawn.

    (e) Giving air time: taking definite action to ensure that everyone's viewpoint is fully heard.

    (f) Suggesting ways of making progress: proposing ways of handling problems and information.

    (g) Maintaining positive energy: drawing attention to behaviour that is undermining group effectiveness.

       (h)   Resource utilization: drawing attention to available resources and assisting in their introduction.

3.   *Capture ideas and action points* Many ideas are produced but never exploited. Ideas should be clearly captured and written down. If action steps are to be taken, the person responsible for implementation must be identified and a mechanism for checking on progress should be determined and mutually accepted.

 ## USING A STRUCTURED APPROACH

Most people intend to work in a structured and systematic way but daily pressures can make this difficult. No structure or system can replace attention, awareness and engagement. Structured approaches need to become so integrated into the personality of a manager that they operate at the same level as intuition. In the same way as a car driver does not need to think about when to press a pedal, the manager needs process management skills woven into the fabric of his/her behaviour. Here are some ideas to help you to be more structured in your problem solving.

1.   Write a sign for your wall, such as STRUCTURED WORKERS DO IT STEP BY STEP.

2.   On a flip chart write eight problem-solving and decision-making steps described earlier to act as a reminder. Use this to structure your meetings.

3.   Regularly review your meetings. Spend time at the end of each meeting asking 'How can we work more effectively?'

4.   Obtain feedback on your style from colleagues, staff specialists or group members who will be able to suggest ways of improving your problem solving and decision making skills.

5.   Record problem solving sessions occasionally. Play the video or sound tape back and make a list of ideas for improvement.

6.   Form a discussion group with two or three colleagues and discuss your experience of problem solving with them. Act as counsellors to one another.

OPPORTUNITY FINDING

Problem solving and decision making are the heart of management. Without competence in all the elements in the process the manager is weakened. Problem solving is sometimes regarded as a negative activity – putting right things which are going wrong. This is an excessively pessimistic views, however, as the same management processes are used to find and capture opportunities to improve.

The interdependence between problems, opportunities and decisions is demonstrated by the following example.

Many American schools of the 1990s experience a range of 'problems': violence, underachieving, teenage pregnancy, disruption and drug taking. Set against these 'problems' are 'opportunities' – ways to use the concern of people to focus energy on improvement.

What needs to be done to mitigate the problems (it may be impossible to eliminate them)? The first step is to find a champion or maybe a group of champions. Little happens unless someone takes charge and drives change. The 'champion' then needs to accomplish four tasks:

1. Complete a full diagnosis of what is going wrong and why.
2. Determine a strategy for dealing with the problem and be able to convince audiences that this is the best way forward.
3. Form powerful alliances with as many opinion leaders as possible (reducing the influences of detractors).
4. Shape a plan with strategies for acquiring resources so that implementation is practical and achievable.

With something as significant as a school system there is a crucial need to develop an overall philosophy to guide the change process. Ideas woven into a philosophy are the precedents of policy.

Problem solvers and decision makers benefit from understanding the power of ideas and the significance of innovation. Often it is easier to define the problem (teenage truancy) than to identify the solution. A single problem may require multiple initiatives sometimes coordinated into an interdependent plan. The skills inherent in managing this process are discussed in Blockage 4, Low Creativity.

Skilful problem solving is a substantial organizational asset. It has been said that the distinguishing characteristic of a successful organization is the capacity to realize opportunities and quickly solve the range of problems that occur. Poor problem-solving and decision-making capacity is a major difficulty for any manager or supervisor and, if widespread, it is a primary organization blockage.

CHARACTERISTICS OF MANAGERS WHO ARE STRUCTURED/UNSTRUCTURED PROBLEM SOLVERS AND DECISION MAKERS

As a summary, the following lists the problem-solving characteristics regularly shown by managers. Unstructured problem-solving and decision-making characteristics are listed on the left and structured problem-solving characteristics are listed on the right.

Unstructured problem solving and decision making	*Structured problem solving and decision making*
Allows problems to remain unresolved	Solves problems as they occur
Uses inappropriate techniques	Chooses appropriate techniques
Uses an unstructured approach	Uses a structured approach
Does not clarify who 'owns' problems	Ensures clear ownership of problems
Works to unclear objectives	Identifies objectives clearly
Has vague criteria for achievement	Sets clear criteria for achievement
Assembles information poorly	Handles information skilfully
Takes ill-considered decisions	Takes well-considered decisions
Is ineffective in planning	Plans effectively
Does not review work	Takes time to review work
Coordinates groups poorly	Coordinates groups effectively

WHEN MANAGERS MOST NEED PROBLEM-SOLVING AND DECISION-MAKING SKILLS

A high level of problem-solving and decision-making skills is required in jobs that involve novel situations, contributions which must be integrated, business objectives to be clarified, compiling information to be analysed, and detailed planning. Every manager needs the capacity to solve the problems that regularly occur but superior problem-solving skills are required wherever innovation or adaptation are regularly taking place. Occupations that need a higher level of problem-solving and decision-making skills include politicians, planners, negotiators, administrators, senior managers, top-ranking military personnel and project specialists.

BLOCKAGE

7

UNCLEAR GOALS

It was a boys' school reunion. The bar was packed with middle-aged men discussing their schooldays. Twenty-five years before they had all been wearing school caps at rakish angles, flicking ink pellets and dozing off in French lessons. Now they were balding, reflective and established.

There were many rich topics of conversation. How marriages had fared, whether children were straight or wayward and what illnesses had struck. Perhaps the most interesting discussion point was how each person's career had developed. Some were resigned to mundane jobs whilst others had risen in their careers to be stars. The heart surgeon was talking to the barman and the security officer chatted to the merchant banker.

As the night wore on a group formed and began to reflect on what had shaped each person's career. One thread emerged clearly. Those who were satisfied with their careers had developed a vision of their own future and thrown themselves (heart and mind) into achievement. The unsatisfied (which included some with exalted jobs) had focused their energies on other things or frittered away their time.

As Bargo put it, 'There are some people, however, who seem magically to take hold of their lives ... The world not only seems to make sense to them, it seems to be made for them ... What is their secret? ... It is that they have a clear idea of what they want and they find a way of obtaining it. They work towards goals and the goals they attain seem to satisfy them; they are not constantly changing direction midstream.'

We need clear and valid goals. In order to cope with the rapidity of change, the breadth of choice and the absence of strong traditional codes, each individual needs to reassess his/her goals both carefully and regularly.

---

[1] M. Bargo Jr, *Choices and Decisions: A guidebook for constructing values*, San Diego, CA, University Associates, 1980.

THE MANAGER'S ROLE IN GOAL SETTING

Achievement requires focus and commitment. Since the manager's job is fundamentally concerned with achievement every manager needs the skills of goal setting to focus energy and resources.

Let us spend a few moments thinking about goals. A goal is a milestone on the road between what is and what could be. It is the management tool used to grasp a vision and transform it into an action plan. Consider the owner of a small fruit and vegetable business in the high street. He sees his turnover dropping year by year as supermarkets erode his markets. One day he walks past a health food store which is heaving with people buying sun-dried apricots and olive paté. His imagination begins to buzz. Maybe he could transform his business from being a traditional greengrocers into a boutique of healthy and exotic foods.

This vision becomes elaborated through debate and watchful observation of rival businesses. Then the time comes to make a commitment. The shopkeeper decides not to transform his business overnight but to allocate 10 per cent of the selling space to new products in line with his new business vision. Now he has a goal – to find products which are attractive, have a high profit margin and are consistent with his broader aims.

Management pundits used to advocate that a sequence of goals needs to be fully preplanned but our shopkeeper knows better. He has to experiment (perhaps with a range of nuts and berries) and, depending on the results of the trial, he will set new goals. A success will accelerate progress whereas a failure will cause urgent reflection and re-experimentation.

The process can be described by a diagram (see Figure 3.)

It does not matter where the manager begins in this cycle. Each step leads on to the next and the process has a living, organic quality. The skilful manager is able to:

❑   Determine opportunities and transform problems into opportunities.
❑   Develop a vision of a better future.
❑   Transform a vision into a manageable process through goal setting.
❑   Make commitment decisions to achieve goals.
❑   Manage the learning process so that the wisdom of goals can be reviewed.

Figure 3 The goal cycle

There is often confusion as to the definition of such words as 'goal', 'task', 'objective', etc. For our definition see Figure 4.

Improving goal setting can be difficult, but it relates intimately to the day-by-day life of the manager.

Try to clarify your own approach to setting goals by answering the following six questions, which are discussed in the remainder of this chapter.

1.   What is my attitude towards goal setting?
2.   What principles do I adopt when goal setting?
3.   How do I set career goals?
4.   How do I set goals at work?
5.   What do I do if things do not work out?
6.   How do I help others set effective goals?

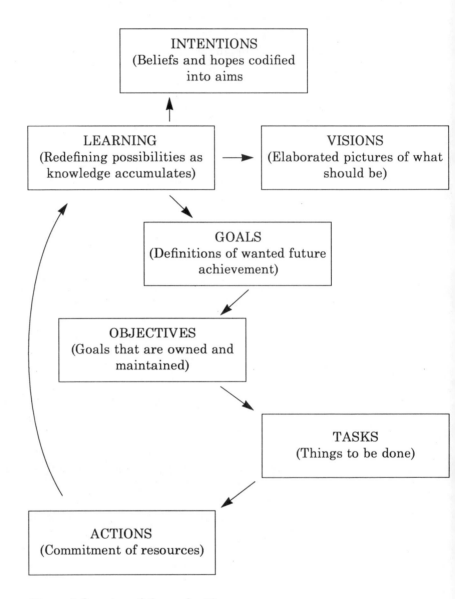

Figure 4 Overview of the goal-setting process

 GOAL SETTING: AN ATTITUDE TO LIFE

Until a few decades ago, it was customary for most people to take their places in society on the basis of tradition and social convention.

The options of a new-born child were to a large extent proscribed because of the strong social influences that shaped the progress of an individual. Although some individuals broke with tradition, becoming artists, entrepreneurs, criminals, and, in a few cases, saints, most followed predictable and conventional living patterns.

People should recognize their own capacities and develop their lives, take opportunities, and be responsible for their own futures. An active and responsible life stance is a vital component of being effective, especially for managers. Herman put it this way: 'It is better by far to help the individual to discover, use and rejoice in his strength and ability and to move forward for himself than to have others pushing his wheelchair for him.'[1]

Without clarity of direction, a manager lacks firmness and resolve. Opportunities may be lost because they are undetected, and trivial distractions may take a disproportionate amount of time while the manager is preoccupied with irrelevant byways. Without criteria to assess possibilities and rank them in importance, it is impossible to use scarce resources effectively.

Setting goals requires a belief in the merits of exercising self-control. Without the capacity to control a situation a goal is a mere pipe-dream. Control means that principles dominate action and aims shape commitments. Consider an ageing film star sitting down to her fiftieth birthday party. She knows that the forces of nature are taking their toll yet control can give stability and even reverse some of the negative effects of late nights, booze and a surfeit of what she calls with a coy smile – 'My little pleasures'.

She will need to control her exercise programme, vitamin intake, posture, calories, and so on. She must define her goals and find ways to monitor success or failure. It is pointless to set targets for calories consumed unless a valid record is kept.

Perhaps the most difficult personal challenge is to manage the different parts of oneself. The self who sits down to establish an exercise regime is a different self from the one who wakes at 5 o'clock on a cold wet morning to go out for a three-mile run.

Some solutions to the 'divided self' problem are:

❑ Publish goals so that they achieve the status of commitments in your life.
❑ Appoint a supervisor as a disciplinarian.
❑ Establish highly visible success criteria.
❑ Punish yourself for failing.

---

[1] S. Herman, 'Notes on Freedom' in J. A. W. Pfeiffer and J. E. Jones (eds), *The 1972 Annual Handbook for Group Facilitators*, San Diego, CA: University Associates, 1972.

- ❏ Set achievable targets so that you can enjoy small wins.
- ❏ Nourish your broad vision so that it remains real and vivid.
- ❏ Save personal energy so that you have sufficient resources to make progress: nothing is more undermining than exhaustion.

 ## PRINCIPLES OF GOAL SETTING

Managers have been encouraged by lecturers in business administration and by proponents of managerial systems such as 'management by objectives' (MBO) to set clear goals for themselves and their subordinates. MBO continues to influence management practice around the world. Not all goals are beneficial since goal setting is, by definition, an excluding process (setting one goal means that another will not be pursued). We need to commit ourselves to goals which are wise, progressive and prudent. The process of selecting goals (called 'judgement') is one of the most difficult to learn since it requires educated intuition as much as astute rational analysis. 'Good' judgement is helped by the following:

- ❏ Check your proposals with others before commitment.
- ❏ Consult widely and deeply.
- ❏ Think about each important issue from several points of view.
- ❏ Write your proposed decisions down.
- ❏ Sleep on important items.
- ❏ Give special care to strategic decisions ('strategic decisions' are those that will have a profound effect).

A goal can be defined as 'a time-bound and measurable achievement area'. These characteristics may be examined in the following goal statements:

- ❏ To weigh 160lb by Christmas
- ❏ To be promoted to general manager by the end of next year
- ❏ To take more risks in my job
- ❏ To jog for 30 minutes four times each week
- ❏ To receive more recognition for my work.

Each of these statements tells us something about what a person wants to accomplish but they vary in two important ways. First, some of the statements indicate a time limit on the accomplishment; other statements are open-ended. Second, some of the statements are very specific ('To jog for 30 minutes four times each week'), but others are more general ('To receive more recognition for my work'). The most useful *complete* goal statements are both specific and time-bounded – they then become 'objectives'.

Just because a goal statement is not time-bounded or precise does not mean that it is defective. Broader statements of intent and vision can be powerful, motivating and positive. However, it is necessary to distinguish between intentions and goals: intentions are pious hopes until they are supported by goal statements, which need to be developed into objectives.

Managers have reported that objectives help to bring about change when they meet the following criteria:

- ❑ Ownership is clear.
- ❑ The owner feels personally committed to achieving the objective.
- ❑ Success criteria are measurable, explicit and possible to meet.
- ❑ Success measures are in place.
- ❑ It is possible to be successful by taking small steps.
- ❑ Time limits and milestones are identified.
- ❑ Clear communication takes place.
- ❑ Review is frequent, serious and formal.

Setting goals structures time. Without goals people are likely to be the victims of chance and servants of the whims of others. Some goals are fundamental and they persist for generations (e.g. to make a profit); other goals are superficial and transient (e.g. to have an enjoyable Christmas party). However, simply having a goal does not offer a magic solution to difficulties. Goals shape the future but because circumstances often change, those established in the past may become irrelevant or unachievable. This is especially true in the politics of senior management, which is the art of the possible. It is said that 'a week is a long time in politics' because new factors can rapidly and radically alter a situation.

 ## HOW TO SET CAREER GOALS

Without clear goals, individuals tend to squander energy on irrelevant pursuits. They may become demoralized and accept uncritically the influence of others. Colleagues can assist in clarifying or setting goals for subordinates but individuals who take responsibility for their own directions and standards feel stronger and are more in control of their own lives. The more they take charge of their actions, the greater their sense of personal dignity.

Even in a volatile and changing environment there are possibilities for career growth and personal achievement. Periodically, it is helpful for managers to review their career goals. This is particularly relevant when some sectors of industry are declining while others thrive. In the next ten years, there will be a whole new range of managerial jobs and many existing functions will become redundant. The prudent manager has placed himself or herself where the industry will develop.

When you review your career goals,[1] bear in mind the following points. First, the organization that employs you may have charted various pathways by which it fills its senior positions. These career routes both extend and limit your choices, unless you choose to change organizations, industries or national boundaries. Second, your personal desires, constraints and talents are extremely relevant to your career. When reviewing your career goals, there are some key questions that need to be answered:

❑ How much of my life do I want my career to occupy?
❑ What income do I wish to achieve?
❑ How important is organizational status to me?
❑ What professional standing do I wish to achieve?
❑ Is it important to me to create something new or different?
❑ Which industries attract me?
❑ What size of organization do I want as an employer?
❑ Which countries do I wish to work in?
❑ What would I like to be remembered for?

After you have considered these questions, you should find that your choices become broader and clearer. This increases the amount of control you have over your future since choices enhance personal power. Although unexpected opportunities may come along and alter your choices, if your broad intent has been established it is easier to determine when to say 'yes' or 'no'.

Use three time frames for goal setting: the next twelve months, the next three years and the next ten years. When you feel ready, try to generate written career goal statements. Have these typed and review them regularly. Once they are recorded, you can check the realism of your goals in two ways:

[1.] For further help on career management see Dave Francis, *Managing Your Own Career*, HarperCollins, 1994.

❏   checking against your history: review your past and examine
      how much you have achieved and developed;
❏   checking with friends: others will know you well and can give
      valuable feedback. Some people who are close to you may have a
      vested interest in casting you in a certain role so their suggestions
      may be based on their needs rather than yours. Balance this by
      soliciting responses from colleagues and professional counsellors.

In summary, the reasons for setting your career goals include the
following:

❏   Career options can be recognized.
❏   You are strengthened in the process.
❏   The relevance of your actions and experiences can be better
      assessed.
❏   Others can be persuaded to support your point of view.
❏   You can gain energy.
❏   You can increase your sense of control and calmness.
❏   The possibility of achieving desired results is increased.

 ## HOW TO SET GOALS FOR YOURSELF

Goal setting is a form of decision making. It is helpful to look at the
process by which goals are determined, validated and activated.

STEP ONE: CLARIFYING A NEED

It is only useful to establish goals when an existing situation is unsatisfactory or can be improved. All humans need to breathe and the
availability of air means that they rarely consider their breathing.
However, people who find themselves trapped in a submerged vehicle
with a shortage of air must immediately set goals to acquire an
adequate supply of air as soon as possible.

Setting goals requires reflection on your present situation and
clarification of what you wish to achieve. This calls for imagination
and depends on freedom from limitations.

STEP TWO: CLARIFYING OPTIONS

There are choices in every sector of life. Some of these may go against your values or cause excessive difficulty to those around you but in theory, at least, the choices are there.

First identify as many options as possible. This can partly be accomplished by private brainstorming but research and the views of others can also be used to expand the list. Take, for example, a person who is thinking of changing careers. The immediate possibilities will probably be identified in jobs similar to the one held, but there are a host of other possibilities. For example you may become a postman, a cook, or a gun-runner. It is not until a full range of options is identified that there is a basis for a wise choice.

STEP THREE: DECIDING WHAT YOU WANT

A list of choices is not enough; you need to know what you are striving toward and wish to accomplish. This may sound straightforward, but determining what you want is not always easy. There are three key questions to be answered:

❑   What is important?
❑   What risks are you prepared to take?
❑   What effects will your decisions have?

Identify those boundaries that affect your choices. You may decide that some options are simply too risky and prefer to pursue safer courses of action. Assessing risk is an important step. The assessment of risk requires analysis of both the costs and the likely prospects of failure. The following simple formula gives a broad framework:

$$\frac{\text{Possible benefits of success}}{\text{Possible risks of failure}} \times \frac{\text{Prospects of success}}{\text{Prospects of failure}} = ?$$

Few individuals are completely free agents. People are usually deeply enmeshed in a network of interconnected relationships and responsibilities. Your decisions affect others and in turn their decisions affect you. This is not to say that you should allow other people's reactions always to stop you from doing what you like. Rather, the best way to deal with an issue is to methodically consider the other people likely to be affected by your decisions and determine whether what you will gain is worth whatever effect it has on them.

Discussing your ideas and possible actions with those likely to be affected and seeing how they react can help you make difficult choices more sensitively.

STEP FOUR: MAKING THE CHOICE

Now that you have identified a range of options and clarified personal needs and wants, you must make the choice. In effect, you are saying that you will devote your energies to one path rather than another. It may be that the other path would have led you to a more satisfying and desirable future. There is no guaranteed technique for eliminating the risks of making incorrect decisions. All you can do is choose the most attractive and promising options and know why you selected them.

STEP FIVE: SETTING OBJECTIVES

Some goals are expressed in general terms, such as 'I want to take more risks in my job'. Such statements are so broad that they are likely to remain pious hopes unless made more concrete. Such goals must be turned into objectives. This enables the 'end game' to be determined and ownership of the initiative to be established.

STEP SIX: ESTABLISHING TIME FRAMES

Objectives become valuable when time frames are established. Often tasks must be established, sequenced and their size and scope determined. When the quantity of work required is determined and assessed in relation to competing demands it becomes possible to move from an objective to a work programme.

STEP SEVEN: MONITORING ACHIEVEMENT

Someone who decides to lose weight will probably set weight-loss goals and begin to diet. One potent source of motivation can be a weight graph displayed on the bathroom wall. As the line recording weekly weight descends, the dieter can glow with satisfaction but, should the line turn upwards, it signals that the dieter's strategy is failing and more discipline or a new diet is required. The benefits of monitoring performance include:

- ❏ Feedback on effectiveness
- ❏ A feeling of success when progress is made
- ❏ A feeling of gloom when failure is experienced
- ❏ An opportunity to review tactics and plan new actions.

Find tools that assess progress, although this may be a harsh discipline. There are some complex objectives that cannot be measured once and for all, but we must try to find valid measures for every managerial initiative.

The seven steps that have been provided can serve as a checklist to help you clarify your goals. By asking yourself which of the steps you often omit or handle inadequately, you gain a framework for re-examining your approach and developing new skills.

 ## HAZARDS

There is a hazard with goal setting: spontaneity and freedom to respond flexibly to situations may be inhibited by a predetermined frame of reference. If rigid goals become an obsession, they inhibit flexibility and learning. Setting goals brings planning into people's lives. Efforts to establish goals should never be allowed to strangle spontaneity and limit freedom to respond to new opportunities. Rather, goals are best framed to enable the individual to be more open to possibilities ahead. If predetermined goals sap the individual's spontaneity, then creativity is replaced by sterile planning.

If you find that your goals are not being fulfilled, use the following checklist to identify the possible causes:

- ❏ *Are your goals really important to you?* Goals that lack genuine commitment are rarely fulfilled.
- ❏ *Are your goals realistic?* Sometimes people set goals that are almost impossible to achieve.
- ❏ *Are you investing sufficient care and energy?* Achievable goals may not be realized because insufficient action was taken to overcome obstacles.
- ❏ *Are the goals still relevant?* New circumstances may have made some of your goals obsolete.
- ❏ *Have you appropriately involved others?* Without help and support, many projects fail. Early communication and engagement increases the probability of achievement.

❑   *Have you given up prematurely?* There are many cases in which someone has 'thrown in the towel' too early, although persistence would have resulted in success.

 ## HELPING OTHERS TO SET GOALS

Managers and supervisors have the important task of clarifying and setting objectives with other people. This is so important that MBO – referred to earlier – was devised to improve the quality of the objective-setting process.

The purpose of MBO is to focus attention on what is achieved, instead of simply tackling tasks. Although MBO promotes detailed thought at senior levels concerning the tangible outcomes that are desired, it leaves decisions about operations to the person on the spot.

Like most management tools, objective setting can be abused but managers should use the benefits of the discipline to energize individuals, reaffirm the meaning of work and use time effectively. Objectives set with others should avoid the following potential pitfalls:

1.   *Lack of realism*   Objectives need to be achievable but they should stretch resources.
2.   *Undefined time frame*   Well-set objectives include a time scale for achievement. They can then be reviewed periodically.
3.   *Unmeasurability*   Wherever possible, objectives are best expressed in terms that can be measured. This permits clear evaluation of accomplishment.
4.   *Non-alignment*   Objectives make sense only when they are aligned with the organizational strategy. Effectiveness, rather than efficiency, is therefore a key criterion. All objectives need to be organizationally relevant.
5.   *Lack of shared commitment*   People who collectively agree to work together in pursuit of a common objective can gain great strength from the group. Objectives are often accepted grudgingly and the energizing vitality of group commitment is not fully harnessed.
6.   *Clash of objectives*   Sometimes individual or group objectives are devised in such a way that they conflict with others. Without mechanisms for working through these conflicts, much effort is wasted.
7.   *Lack of communication*   Organizations are vulnerable to breakdowns in communication. Directors establish objectives, often

expressed in financial terms, and then communicate them in ways which do not enthuse employees. Objectives gain strength as they are shared.

8. *Use as punishment* Setting objectives can be used as a strategy for hunting individuals and punishing them. This is a negative use.

9. *Lack of review* A major benefit of objective setting is that it provides a framework for systematic review. Individuals can learn through counselling on their success in accomplishing objectives.

Objectives provide directions in which to travel. It is helpful to imagine a large ocean-going vessel with all the facilities needed to move huge loads from one continent to another. The ship could not progress without a rudder. Objectives are the rudders of individual and group activity. Without them capacity is underdirected and, consequently, squandered.

CHARACTERISTICS OF MANAGERS WITH CLEAR/UNCLEAR GOALS

It is our observation that managers who have unclear goals exhibit the characteristics listed here on the left and those with clear goals exhibit the characteristics listed on the right:

Confused personal goals	*Clear personal goals*
Does not specify personal aims	Specifies personal aims
Tends to change direction	Maintains continuity
Fails to measure progress	Assesses progress frequently
Avoids time frames	Sets time boundaries
Is unclear about options	Explores options
Takes unconsidered risks	Takes calculated risks
Accepts vague objectives	Clarifies objectives
Fails to balance personal/work aspects	Maintains satisfactory personal/work balance
Does not plan career progression	Plans career progression
Lacks skill in setting objectives	Is skilled in objective setting
Does not share aims with others	Shares aims with others
Does not delegate effectively	Delegates effectively
Assesses subordinates subjectively	Assesses subordinates objectively

WHEN MANAGERS MOST NEED CLEAR GOALS

All managers need skills in goal setting. As responsibilities and status grow so does the need to become proficient in this basic skill. Supervisors usually need to set goals to accomplish defined tasks whereas more senior managers become concerned with wider aspects, like values, strategies, competences and organization principles. Hence the importance of a process of goal setting which must be dynamic, open and realistic. If managers have this skill they have made a giant step towards true accomplishment.

8

NEGATIVE MANAGEMENT STYLE

At an international business school, a group of middle-aged managers assembled for a lecture. They were assertive survivors who had been selected for promotion into powerful positions at the hubs of their organizations. Their conversations ranged from business process re-engineering to deep-sea fishing.

The lecturer entered and said: 'Today we are going to move away from techniques and look at more fundamental values. I should like to use imagination as a tool and ask you to close your eyes and try to clear your mind of distracting thoughts.' The managers appeared apprehensive, shuffled a little, then sat back quietly and closed their eyes.

The lecturer continued: 'I want you to imagine that you have been summoned by a leading politician to a plush central government office. Picture yourself waiting outside the door. Now you enter and sit down. The politician says to you, "The government is considering a most important and well-paid project for you. We want you to organize and manage an entirely new factory to make antigravity mats. The mats have just been secretly perfected and patented – they will help our economy enormously. There is one condition for your appointment to this position: the plant must be perfectly managed. You can do anything you want, except pay people excessively. Tell me how you would manage the plant. I want to know the fundamental principles you intend to employ."'

The lecturer went on: 'Now, in your mind's eye, conduct the conversation with the politician and tell him how you would run the plant. In a few minutes we shall discuss your ideas.' There was silence in the group as each manager conducted an imaginary dialogue.

The lecturer called the managers back to reality and began to collect their ideas and chart them on a whiteboard. The statements listed included:

- ❏ A lively environment
- ❏ Teamwork
- ❏ High standards expected
- ❏ Open management style
- ❏ Continuous improvement ethic
- ❏ Massive use of information technology
- ❏ Process management
- ❏ Autonomous work groups

❑   Total quality management
❑   Lean manufacturing principles

After the lecturer had collected about sixty statements, he began to group them into categories. They conveniently divided into three sections: (1) organizational structure and communication, (2) management style and controls, and (3) healthy and energetic culture. It was apparent that some participants felt very differently about the same issues.

'Now', the lecturer said, 'let us examine this list and try to pick out the underlying values and beliefs that are implicit in the statements you have made. You see, each of us has beliefs about good and bad ways to manage. Often, we don't explore our assumptions. The exercise you have just completed helps to identify the values on which you base your personal managerial philosophy.'

As the discussion continued, each manager began to question personal values and beliefs. The session concluded with these remarks: 'There are no right or wrong answers. Different managerial philosophies have worked well in the same situation. There is always a choice about the appropriate management philosophy for the time.'

In this blockage chapter, individual managerial philosophies are examined in some depth. The concern here is not to look at day-to-day managerial skills, as these are dealt with elsewhere in this book. The material is presented in two main sections. The first considers the managerial group as a whole and reviews how a progressive corporate philosophy can be developed. The second focuses on the individual manager and developing a personal management philosophy that is mature, effective and positive.

 CORPORATE MANAGERIAL PHILOSOPHY

Management groups adapt their philosophies considerably to suit their organization and the culture in which they operate. In our experience, the most important factors in an organization's management philosophy are: (1) the economic fortunes of the enterprise, (2) the technology of the industry, and (3) the personal beliefs of its leaders.

Management is a complex field that is susceptible to fads and fashions. The fashion cycle in management thinking has advantages. Ideas can be compared to radioactive substances: they decay in potency and lose their vitality over a period of time. Therefore, new ideas are essential to prevent sterility and ossification. Also, ideas become popular because they meet a need of the time.

However, the tendency of organizations to embrace the latest management gimmick has led managers and supervisors to justified cynicism as each year's great new idea is presented to them. They may listen attentively, while saying to themselves: 'We've heard it all before: it will be a nine-day wonder.' Although managements need to keep open to current thinking, indiscriminate experimentation is distracting. It is just as useful to evaluate an idea and discard it for good reason as to adopt a suggestion. The benefit comes from reflection and review.

Most management theorists work in a similar way. They analyse situations, develop or adapt concepts and test them wherever they can. Research is usually conducted in sophisticated businesses that are accustomed to allowing eminent specialists to examine their organizational entrails. Then a theory is polished and packaged before its presentation. The resulting product may become a gigantic money maker or fail to raise a spark of enthusiasm. Because the new management ideas are largely developed in enlightened environments, the relevance of the ideas to the vast bulk of organizations is rarely tested. This makes it impossible blindly to accept outside guidance; all philosophies and theories need to be checked for relevance.

The word relevance is key. Some philosophies of management would be functional in a science laboratory in California but would be ridiculous in a haggis factory in Scotland. Each theory and value judgement must be assessed in relation to its relevance to a particular organization at a particular time. This is not a 'once-only' consideration. Regular review is necessary to ensure that management philosophy is up to date and well communicated. When this is done the firm is on the road to becoming a 'learning organization'.

BLOCKAGES TO ORGANIZATIONAL EFFECTIVENESS

Organizations are so complex and varied that it is difficult to develop a comprehensive and useful assessment of organizational well-being. However, managers need frameworks to help them collect data and understand where potential weaknesses occur. We advocate that managers should investigate twelve key elements that can block an organization's effectiveness.[1] Each of these potential blockages is relatively distinct and, taken together, they provide a comprehensive view of the human side of an organization. The blockages occur without the following:

1. *Effective recruitment and selection*   The new people who are employed by an organization are capable of developing necessary

---

[1] See the authors' *Unblocking Your Organization* (Gower, 1990).

skills quickly, have a positive attitude, possess core competences and are able to grow with the firm.

2. *Clear organization structure*   The allocation of power, lines of responsibility and roles provides a flexible organization structure appropriate to the technologies that the firm operates.

3. *Adequate control*   Individuals have a clear direction and purpose to their work, which they fully understand. Control is in the hands of those who have the necessary information. Excessive direction is avoided.

4. *Good training*   People quickly learn new skills and keep up to date with the advances in their fields. Competences are developed for tomorrow's organization.

5. *High motivation*   The general level of vitality and energy in the organization is high. People are willing to be active and this is channelled into the achievement of corporate objectives.

6. *Practical creativity*   Ideas are generated and carefully sifted for application. New ideas are practically applied and tested. The organization is capable of managing innovation both technically and organizationally. The firm is 'ahead of the field'.

7. *Good teamwork*   People work well together. They quickly form effective teams that use the resources available, produce results and use time wisely. Relationships are open and inter-group linkages are actively managed.

8. *Mature management philosophy*   The members of senior management have thought through their management styles, and clarified organizational guidelines. The management philosophy they have adopted is humane, consistent, effective and widely practised. Managers take their responsibilities seriously and validate the soundness of their beliefs.

9. *Developed management resource*   The organization realizes that sufficient management resources are essential to survival. Important future staffing needs are identified and prepared for in good time. Managers are stimulated by current management thinking in other organizations.

10. *Lucid aims*   The organization has clarified its broad objectives and defined its mission. These aims have been expressed in terms each member of the workforce can understand. Strategic intent guides opportunism.

11. *Fair rewards*   Those who make the highest contribution to the health of the enterprise get the highest rewards. Payment systems are generally felt to be fair and equitable within wider economic constraints. Besides feeling that financial rewards are adequate, people feel that their work is appreciated and they receive psychological rewards for their efforts.

12. *Positive individual development* Individuals are developed within the organization. Their skills and contribution are developed so that broad competence is achieved. High personal effectiveness becomes the tradition of the organization.

The absence of these attributes constitutes a 'blockage'. Listed as above, they help to make sense of the complex intertwining of behaviours that give an organization its distinctive character. Because exact measurement of such factors is rarely possible, skilful managers and supervisors place much trust in their 'feel' for what is going on. The competent manager will assess the range of tangible and intangible factors that are significant, pick out the key 'levers for change' and make decisions that frequently produce the predicted results. A coherent philosophy underlies the manager's individual decisions. Results can take a long time to emerge, so the insightful manager spends much of his time building for the future.

BUILDING A POSITIVE WORK CLIMATE

Positive managers and supervisors invest much of their energy in striving to create an organizational climate that is conducive to accomplishing results, allows problems to be resolved and facilitates positive change. The concept of climate may be clarified with a negative example. How many times have you gone into a shop as a customer and been treated as though you were an interruption to the employees' work rather than the purpose of it? Did they act sullenly, move with infuriating slowness, displaying a lack of interest that signalled to the world that they would much rather be elsewhere? Did you get the impression that if you happened to be in the doorway at closing time, you would be trampled as the staff rushed to escape? This shop has developed a negative climate which probably pervades every aspect of its work. There may be brilliant systems in such an organization, but the attitudes of its people undermine its effectiveness. The attitudes of employees both respond to and create a group or organizational climate.

It is helpful to think of group climate in terms of flows of human energy. People are capable of devoting energy to satisfying their needs or responsibilities. When the people described in the example were behaving like unwilling captives, they were failing to express their latent energy and vitality. The goal of an insightful manager is to liberate the positive energy of subordinates and channel its expression toward the achievement of organizational goals. This expresses, in the jargon of management science, the manager's concern with the 'motivation' of employees. Motivation is related to energy and, from the management point of view, individuals can use their energy in the following three ways:

1. *Positively* These individuals are in touch with their personal energy and can cope with the inevitable setbacks that occur. They are committed to accomplishment and are disposed to work toward the achievement of organizational objectives. The success of the enterprise is seen as worthwhile and important.

2. *Negatively* These individuals are in touch with their energy but focus on organizationally destructive achievement. The expression of energy undermines organizational capacity. Too much time is spent on grumbling, retaliation and hostility. The achievement of organizational goals is seen to be irrelevant or insignificant.

3. *Blocked* These individuals are out of touch with their own reservoir of vitality and energy. They can no longer find and express themselves. Such people may be so rigid and pessimistic in outlook that they are unable to devote themselves wholeheartedly to the accomplishment of any objectives. Blocked energy is often associated with low job interest and unfulfilled career aspirations.

Human energy is probably the most important resource available to management. Managers and supervisors would like their employees to use their energy positively and make a maximum contribution to the goals of their organization. If an organization can liberate a groundswell of favourable attitudes from its employees, then it reaps the rewards in thousands of ways every week. Military leaders know that a soldier who has no personal commitment will have little personal pride and, more significantly, will lack the will to win battles. The importance of harnessing people's energy has been described so often that is unnecessary to repeat it here. However, less clearly explored are the factors that reduce or block the expression of positive energy within organizations. There are no fixed solutions to such problems. Much depends on the history of the organization, the locality, and the type of people employed. Operating a factory in Tokyo, Japan, is a very different matter from operating one in Liverpool, England.

MOTIVATION

Motivation can be seen as a double concept; it is a complex topic. Certain factors, which may be called *motivation limiters*, need to be resolved or they will lead to dissatisfaction. Other factors, *key motivators*, actually increase the output of energy and are genuine sources of personal satisfaction. We can review organizations with the following two objectives in mind:

1. To reduce the level of demotivation by reducing the motivation limiters

2. To increase the level of motivation by enhancing the key motivators.

The following section describes six factors that are relevant to motivation. As you read them, you may find it helpful to reflect on which are motivation limiters and which are key motivators. Some of our own findings are described at the end of the section.

1. *Work environment*   There is no doubt that the environment in which work takes place can influence the attitudes and energy of the workers. This means that it pays an organization to invest time, resources and interest in developing an environment that helps accomplish the organization's task and meets the needs of the employees. We have seen many examples of people being 'turned off' by their working environments, from a technician located in a noisy production line to a teacher in an unresourced classroom.

2. *Remuneration*   Remuneration includes wages and salaries, holidays and fringe benefits. The philosophy underlying remuneration is key. Do you pay people for responsibility? For qualifications? For skills? For performance? For potential? Each payment principle has strengths and weaknesses. In general, the shift is towards locally determined pay achieved for results.

3. *Security*   We are changing our attitudes to security, seeing the concept more as an inner quality rather than a job for life. Feelings of security are not simply about having or not having a job. People also fear the loss of position and the esteem in which they are held by others. Most people like to feel secure in the working group to which they belong, which makes the development of teamwork important.

4. *Personal development and growth*   One of the most effective ways of enhancing the contribution of people in an organization is to facilitate their personal development. Development and experience are inseparable and, although training and education help, there is no substitute for facilitating learning by increasing responsibility and providing new experiences. Linked closely with the development of people is feedback on their performance, which can be one of the strongest motivators to even greater accomplishment.

5. *Involvement*   Most people like to know that their job is useful and want to feel part of the organization that employs them. Some organizations present information to employees in a straightforward way that helps them to make sense of what is happening. Others, however, seem to go to great lengths to keep

their employees in the dark. Because involvement is a two-way process, employees need to be asked for their opinions, suggestions and views. Groups usually have an 'opinion leader' – one person who is the most influential – and it is particularly important that this person be involved and persuaded to support management objectives.

6.   *Interest and challenge*   The need to achieve significant results is widely spread throughout most organizations. Most people seek work that offers them some challenge, requires skills and is not too easy to accomplish. The content of a job itself can energize an employee. It is unfortunate that far too many jobs are tedious and undemanding. There is a story that in one organization a visitor saw an operator performing the most basic of routine tasks on the production line. The visitor said, 'Why, that job is so simple, a monkey could do it!' The operator looked at the visitor and said, 'That's not true. The monkey would be bored to death!' Much can be done to examine the way in which jobs are organized and the extent to which they offer interest and challenge. Even apparently menial jobs, like sweeping and shelf-filling, can often be redesigned to make them more satisfying.

MOTIVATION LIMITERS AND KEY MOTIVATORS

Our studies have shown that the factors described in items 1, 2 and 3 in the above list act principally as demotivators when employees are dissatisfied with them; they will block others' attempts to increase motivation. These are the motivation limiters.

On the other hand, items 4, 5 and 6 are the factors that really motivate people and produce much achievement in organizations. These are the key motivators.

Management is a collective function within an organization. It acts as a body, making collective decisions and seeking common perceptions about needs and problems. Within this context managers act independently, allowing their individual personalities and experiences to assist their decision making. Without this freedom to express individual character, much of the vitality and colour of an enterprise would be lost. The insightful manager can contribute a great deal to effective management thinking within an organization. The following are some ways in which individual managers can help to develop a mature management philosophy:

❏   Reviewing current strengths and weaknesses
❏   Providing frameworks to aid understanding

❑ Introducing new perspectives
❑ Providing a forum for debate
❑ Collecting data on attitudes
❑ Analysing present management style
❑ Developing new concepts and ideas.

 INDIVIDUAL MANAGERIAL PHILOSOPHY

For many decades, managers and behavioural scientists have worked at identifying the characteristics of effective management practice. They have recorded and analysed the ways in which effective and ineffective managers perform their daily tasks. The differences in performance have been documented and the conclusion of many specialists is that a core managerial quality is direct leadership. Studies of leadership are summarized here in an effort to reveal their increasing relevance and practicality.

THE DEVELOPING THEORY OF LEADERSHIP

In the 1940s, millions of men and women were called into the armed forces to undertake difficult, dangerous and crucial tasks with a minimum of training. Psychologists also became part of the military forces, and they were set to work to study officers and military teams to identify the characteristics that made units successful. Leadership style of managers and commanders ranged from autocratic at one end of a behavioural scale to democratic at the other. The autocratic leader directed, controlled, specified requirements and punished if things went awry. The democratic leader shared information, collected ideas, checked for consensus, considered proposals and used group pressure to control individuals.

Leaders in business organizations were also studied in depth and social scientists reported that leadership influence has two primary sources: (1) an individual's influence exemplified by the power implicit in his/her particular job or role; and (2) each individual's personal influence and power. It seemed clear to the researchers that leadership style was a function partly of position and partly of personality. Later, they learned that many more influences were at work, including the expectations of others, the character of the job, the expectations of supervisors, trade union attitudes, governmental legislation and so on.

In the 1960s researchers intensified their studies of managers at work. They observed that some managers devote little of their time to encouraging, supporting and developing relationships, whilst others perform these functions to a considerable extent. As these primary management styles were identified, the social scientists made a prediction: some people were very active in trying to get the job done; others in trying to form good relationships – but it would be the manager who balanced both who would be the most successful.

In time, this simple hypothesis was not verified in practice. What did seem true was that different styles of management could work in some settings but not in others. By the 1990s it was clear that there was no single best approach that could be used universally: different organizational settings required different approaches. The new prediction became: the manager whose style was most appropriate for a particular group would most likely succeed in achieving high output.

RECENT LEADERSHIP IDEAS

In recent years more attention has been paid to identifying the needs of an individual situation and then determining a suitable leadership style. Consider the case of a group of managers from a factory. One of them is responsible for quality control, another is installing a new production line, a third is supervising a group of new recruits workers and a fourth is managing a long-established packing department. Each of these managers and supervisors works in a different environment, completing particular tasks with a unique group of people. Also their competence and capability vary. It would be naive to suppose that each manager could use an identical style. Leadership style has to vary because the needs of the subordinate are different. Hence, an important question is: 'What style of leadership does this person need from me?'

Behavioural science placed extreme importance on the development of rapport, consultation and personal liking between a manager and his subordinates. This emphasis on human relations served as an antidote to the exploitative and mechanistic views of traditional managerial activities. Telling people what to do, disciplining them, and taking a firm stand were often considered to be symptoms of inadequate management. Some experienced managers and supervisors have cast a jaundiced eye at this 'new-fangled' philosophy because they believe that there is a place for strong management. With experience we have learned that managers were right to question the assumption that participative management was the only answer.

SITUATIONAL LEADERSHIP

Managerial science has caught up with management practice in the situational leadership model developed by Paul Hersey and Kenneth Blanchard.[1] Their approach is valued as practical and relevant by many managers. According to their view, an effective manager learns to diagnose the leadership needs of complex situations and skilfully applies the appropriate style. We have drawn from Hersey and Blanchard in describing the following four styles of management behaviour.

Telling

What it is
The leader instructs carefully and watches task performance, remaining very involved in the detail of what is going on. Inadequate performance and unsatisfactory standards are quickly identified and pointed out to the person held responsible. The leader makes it clear what is expected and insists on improvement, placing emphasis on individual skill development.

When to use it
The Telling style of leadership is applied to individuals and groups who are unable to tackle the task and lack the will to learn for themselves. The approach is especially useful with new recruits or when taking over departments that have been allowed to 'go to seed'.

What to do

- ❑ Be clear about your standards
- ❑ Instruct extensively
- ❑ Develop individual's technical skills
- ❑ Check performance
- ❑ Discipline when necessary
- ❑ Point out errors and good work
- ❑ Develop pride in good performance
- ❑ Be considerate but firm
- ❑ Emphasize performance
- ❑ Help learning by showing interest in learning problems.

---

[1] Paul Hersey and Kenneth Blanchard, *Management of Organisational Behaviour* (3rd ed.), Englewood Cliffs, NJ: Prentice Hall, 1977.

Selling

What it is

The leader takes frequent initiatives and is very active in directing, instructing and monitoring performance. Communication is given a high priority and the leader invests energy in getting acquainted with individuals and in developing rapport with them. Much attention is given to performance standards and the employees are involved in setting them. The relevance of people's work is discussed, and their performance is related to the organization.

When to use it

The Selling leadership style is used with more established groups and individuals with certain basic skills but still much to learn. The style is well suited to groups whose members are willing but need to care more about their work. The Selling approach is also useful with groups that have quality or production problems they are unable to solve. The leader's emphasis on control and instruction develops workers' skills in a systematic manner.

What to do

- ❑ Spend time with each individual
- ❑ Identify topics of common interest ˙
- ❑ Assess individual character
- ❑ Communicate extensively
- ❑ Develop pride in output
- ❑ Be directive whenever necessary
- ❑ Monitor performance according to standards
- ❑ Discipline to maintain standards
- ❑ Reward positive behaviour

Participating

What it is

The leader focuses on improving the morale and spirit of the group and is active in developing personal relationships and encouraging participation. People are taught to tackle and solve their own problems. Direction is kept to a minimum, although exceptional circumstances are clarified and decided by the manager. Care is taken to see that important decisions are fully explained, and the leader encourages the group members to make a contribution to the wider organization.

When to use it

The Participating leadership style is used with individuals and groups who have the basic skills and competence to handle most of the technical aspects of the job. Further development of such a group requires that the members take more responsibility for their day-to-day work and keep their own morale high.

What to do

- ❏ Limit direction and control
- ❏ Set up self-monitoring systems
- ❏ Counsel on problems
- ❏ Develop people by coaching assignments
- ❏ Communicate widely
- ❏ Encourage comment and feedback
- ❏ Communicate objectives without specifying how they will be achieved
- ❏ Give increasing responsibility.

Delegating

What it is
The leader acts as a resource but leaves much of the work to the individual group members. Day-to-day monitoring and control are administered by the group members.

When to use it
The Delegating leadership style is used with individuals or groups who have achieved a competent level of skills and are willing to devote their energies to doing a good job. The style is appropriate to managing competent people who have responsible and positive attitudes toward their organizations.

What to do

- ❏ Clarify and agree objectives
- ❏ Give support when requested
- ❏ Represent the group to others if necessary
- ❏ Avoid interfering
- ❏ Respond to requests seriously.

DEVELOPMENTAL STAGES

Individuals and groups go through a number of development stages, and the good leader will identify what is needed at each stage. This process is more complex than it appears. The concept of maturation of personality is a useful aid to understanding individual and organizational needs. Some individuals lack either the willingness or the ability to learn a job or to handle it. The style of leadership appropriate for them is very different from that required by willing and able people.

Similar developmental stages can be observed in an individual and a group. The good leader helps a group progress to a high level of responsibility and competence. To do this, he/she will want to know: (1) where the group's development is at the moment; (2) how the group is likely to progress; and (3) what the leader can do to help.

A group can be in one of the four positions shown in Figure 5.

Groups develop slowly and their development can lapse. However, almost all groups can be helped and encouraged to progress to a higher level of maturity. As control and instruction are decreased, the behaviour of the group members needs to be watched to see that they take responsibility and perform well. The process is shown in Figure 6.

THE LEADER'S PERSONALITY

It is the behaviour of a group leader that has been examined here, rather than the personal values implicit in the leader's behaviour. The style adopted by a leader is influenced by many factors, such as local traditions, technology, trade unions, the expectations of senior managers and company history. Although all these factors, and more, affect a leader's behaviour, the leader must retain personal integrity and resist the pressures to play a role. Mechanistic leadership styles lack vitality and engender hostility.

We have concluded, therefore, that insightful leadership meets the needs of people, is appropriate to their personalities and to their level

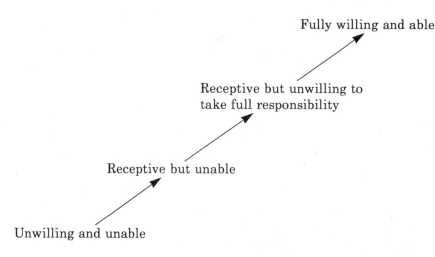

Figure 5 Stages in group development

MATURITY LEVEL
OF WORK GROUP

APPROPRIATE
LEADERSHIP STYLE

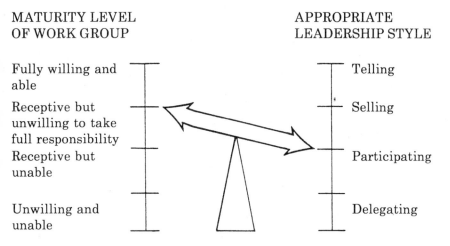

Fully willing and
able

Receptive but
unwilling to take
full responsibility

Receptive but
unable

Unwilling and
unable

Telling

Selling

Participating

Delegating

Figure 6 Appropriate leadership style for maturity level of work group

of job competence, and is also a genuine expression of a manager's personal beliefs. Trying to assume a style that is foreign to your personality is usually a mistake. However, it is possible to learn how to present different aspects of yourself and to discriminate when these are useful and appropriate. A delicate balance is required to avoid manipulation and a false stance of superiority, since such behaviours provoke group members to view the leader with resentment and lack of trust. Always consider the needs of the people being managed. Sometimes they need to be supported, sometimes directed, sometimes disciplined, and sometimes faced with unpleasant information about their behaviour. Their skills, morale and sense of group identity are greatly affected by the way their manager chooses to behave toward them.

Leadership, like honour, is hard to define with precision. Different approaches to leadership are adopted for reasons of personal preference, local custom, and the nature of the tasks being performed and the people performing them. One manager may display symbols of an elevated status – lush carpets, longer lunch breaks, and an immaculately groomed and underworked secretary. Another may exhibit an open style toward subordinates, welcoming direct expression and scorning status symbols that act as barriers. Differences and problems can become sources of strength if they are dealt with openly. It is a primary task of managers and supervisors to ensure that this process happens and that issues are raised, clarified and worked through to resolution.

We have identified an important distinction between the function of manager and leader. The leadership role in a work group may not be one that is necessarily held continuously by a single person.

Well-developed groups have a shared knowledge of the individual strengths of their members and rearrange their resources to suit the task at hand. Hence, it is quite possible that the leadership of groups and committees is changed as different people come to the fore at times when their strengths are needed. This healthy process can be obstructed by a manager who refuses to relinquish information and control. Paradoxically, the formal manager often serves best by partially releasing the right to decide and execute.

 ## CHARACTERISTICS OF MANAGERS WITH NEGATIVE/POSITIVE STYLE

Managers and supervisors who have a positive management style tend to exhibit the characteristics listed here on the right-hand side. Those with a negative management style are more accurately described by the behaviours listed on the left-hand side.

Negative management style	*Positive management style*
Rarely discusses management principles	Frequently discusses management principles
Is unaware of ideas on management style	Is familiar with ideas on management style
Follows fashionable managerial fads	Questions fashionable managerial fads
Does not analyse own weaknesses	Analyses own weaknesses
Creates a negative work climate	Builds a positive work climate
Fails to channel energy	Releases blocked energy
Lacks a realistic theory of motivation	Holds a realistic theory of motivation
Lacks knowledge of own leadership style	Is aware of own leadership style
Maintains fixed leadership style	Varies leadership style according to need
Fails to achieve good performance	Pulls the best out of people
Plays a manipulative role while managing	Shows an authentic management style

WHEN MANAGERS MOST NEED A POSITIVE MANAGEMENT STYLE

Insight into management style and practice is needed by all managers whose jobs require them to directly control subordinates. Such managers have to cope with people of varying talents or levels of ability and with problems of discipline and morale. When an organization is questioning its traditional approach to management and is developing more progressive approaches, its managers particularly need to understand issues of management style. This is of most importance for those in senior positions because they affect management practice throughout their organizations.

POOR ORGANIZING SKILLS

Glasses of champagne were raised in the boardroom. It was such an ecstatic party that even the chairman smiled as a jar of olives cascaded over the walnut boardroom table. The words heard around the boardroom were pregnant with hope: 'turnaround', 'breakthrough', 'the big one', 'triumph'.

Eventually the managing director banged a glass with his Mont Blanc pen and announced, in that lyrical fumbling style that goes hand in hand with too much champagne, 'This is the greatest night in the history of our company [applause]. We've won the Malaysian tunnel contract and work starts tomorrow. It's a high-tech job, plenty of geotechnical puzzles but our design team (thanks to Darren and Helen) have killed the opposition. All those nights drinking sundowners in KL have paid off. We saw it, we claimed it, we won it. The rest is easy.'

A year later the managing director watched as the walnut table was taken from the boardroom – it had been sold along with the other office equipment by order of the administrators of this now bankrupt company. A forlorn group gathered for the last time in the boardroom. Someone had brought a crate of champagne but no one wanted to wash away their disappointment with alcohol. The conversation took the form of a post-mortem. Eventually one of the project managers gained the attention of the group and said quietly, 'I know it's the last time we'll be together as a team and I want to say that it was no one's fault. The job was too big, too many things to take care of at once, too little foreknowledge of the snags. Once things started to drift we should have seen it earlier. But this is all hindsight.' With that the managing director breathed a heavy sigh and replied, 'I remember dancing on this table a year ago because we had won the big one. What let us down was poor management. Our plans were naive, we effected them with more enthusiasm than discipline and we bungled the job. The saddest thing was that it was all unnecessary. Our tender price was right, we had the skills but it all slipped away. We had the will but not the organization. That was the missing link that killed us!'

Management requires a diffuse set of skills but the primary requirement is organizing ability. Without organization energies are dissipated and little is achieved. In this chapter we begin by exploring the nature of the organizing process and then consider the role of the manager as an organizer.

ORGANIZING – BRINGING ORDER TO COMPLEXITY

Perhaps the main task of most managers is organizing. It is in this dimension of management that the role goes beyond leadership (visioning and energizing) into administration (creation and deployment of resources).

Organizing is a complex task made more demanding because it is never completed. A firm is never organized; it is always in the process of organizing. The key elements of organizing are:

1. Conceptualizing the Grand Task
2. Chunking
3. Resource creation
4. Resource alignment and balancing
5. Continuous improvement

We shall examine these five elements in more detail.

CONCEPTUALIZING THE GRAND TASK

Management requires taking decisions within the context of the larger organization. The following story makes the point.

A passenger aircraft developed a fault at Las Vegas airport and mechanics discovered that the replacement would have to come from San Francisco with a trained fitter to complete the installation. The chief engineer received a telephone call at about 3.30pm and decided to send the fitter with the part early the next day. A subsequent review identified that the cost of keeping the plane in Las Vegas (another plane had to be rented to maintain schedules) was about $55,000. So why had the chief engineer not sent his specialist fitter that afternoon? The reason was that a fitter leaving at that time would need overnight accommodation in Las Vegas and the chief engineer's hotel budget was exhausted. He took the 'logical' decision – send the man in the morning. The total cost to the airline of this decision? $54,700 and the indefinable loss of goodwill with all those angry passengers feeling cheated and distressed.

Ideally every manager and supervisor, no matter how lowly, should made decisions as if he or she ran the company. Of course, this is easier said than done. The reward system, particularly the criteria chosen for performance-related pay, shapes attitudes and often focuses on narrow, measurable success criteria. How can junior managers see their roles in the context of the enterprise as a whole? There are eight primary management techniques available:

1. Development of a comprehensive, strategic and tactical vision at the top of the organization.
2. Full and effective communication of the corporate vision down to the lowest levels.
3. A system of management by objective (MBO) which encompasses junior managers' objectives.
4. A reward system which supports those who meet corporate goals.
5. A participative engaging and empowering management style that helps people feel involved.
6. Training of managers to set their objective within the context of broad goals.
7. The identification and honouring of heroes who support the company's broad aims.
8. Deliberate rejection of those who seek to undermine or ignore the 'corporation comes first' principle.

Taken together these techniques are sufficient to align individuals to corporate goals in organizations which have built a high degree of trust between workforce and management. Without that basis of trust any management initiative is undermined.

CHUNKING

Grand Tasks cannot be achieved without 'chunking' – breaking them down into bite-sized chunks. Even though it is ecologically irresponsible to contemplate, it is said that the way to eat an elephant is a spoonful at a time.

Managers are generally experienced in chunking since it is often a daily preoccupation. Consider, for example, a manager of hospital buildings who receives an objective to upgrade the security.

This is a big task and must be chunked. Conceptually an interesting 'how' diagram can be drawn as in Figure 7.

Each of the second level of 'hows' can be expanded. Consider for example 'visit other hospitals'. By asking the question 'how?' against this task we will uncover the third level of tasks, as in Figure 8.

As the subordinate levels of task are identified they must:

❑ Be clearly stated as objectives
❑ Have success criteria attached to them
❑ Have an owner – someone accountable
❑ Be integrated so that coordination is achieved.

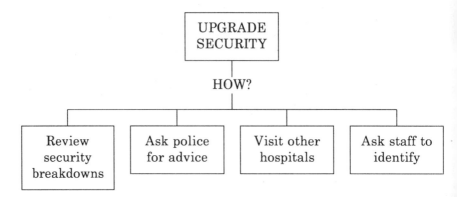

Figure 7 The first stage of a 'how' diagram

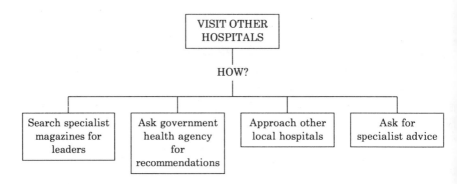

Figure 8 The second stage of a 'how' diagram

RESOURCE CREATION

Resources may exist ready to use. You need a package sent around the world? Call FedEx and a friendly honed international courier service will be at your service. In your organization the print room and the post room are, it is hoped, ready and waiting for your requests.

Resources may exist but you may not be aware of them. Assume that you want to make a video film of the work system in your kitchen. You probably will not know of a reliable, talented, affordable video film maker. One has to be found and so you must begin a process of searching.

Within an organization resources are constantly being created, renewed, transformed and sustained. At the simplest level, each employee is a resource. Investment in the development of individuals to help them acquire relevant competences is a profound commitment. In effect, the manager is perceiving each employee as someone capable of progressive development – it is the manager's job to provide a context which increases the likelihood that people will develop.

There are many more resources than individual talent. A team is a resource; so is a network, a positive climate, a communication process, a high energy level, and an enabling organizational structure. The manager should ask:

❏   What resources would help the task?
❏   How developed are these resources at the moment?
❏   What resource development requirement would it make sense to fill first?
❏   How can the needed resources be developed?
❏   What management initiatives need to be taken now?

RESOURCE ALIGNMENT AND BALANCING

A resource may exist but be unusable because it is unsupported or undirected. Consider a university with a number of talented researchers in biochemistry. The existence of a collection of able researchers is necessary but not sufficient to ensure first-rate research and teaching. Other resources are needed, including:

❏   A fine laboratory
❏   Cash
❏   Able students
❏   Management support
❏   Interesting courses.

These resources are like the links in a chain – each is necessary and the strength of the chain is a function of all the links. Researchers need laboratories and laboratories need cash. Every human system is the same: there must be an integrated set of resources which meets the needs of the situation.

The design of resource systems is a creative task. How does an army commander put together the resources to fight an urban war in an African country or combat a group of terrorists who seek to blow up oil installations? In most cases, there is an accumulated history which can be built upon. But many situations have unique features, perhaps driven by new technology. The science of administration used to be regarded as a dull and obscure subject but we now understand that it is at the core of management practice.

Alignment and balancing of different resources is a challenging management task. Consider, for example, a telephone company that is introducing a new video and home entertainment system. What resources are required? There are many: technical, logistical, financial, marketing, design, procurement and so on. Each resource must be adequate and some might need to be world-class. Each resource needs, like the sections of an orchestra, to be aligned to deliver the project. If any resource is limited or overloaded it will act as a blockage and impair the performance of the system as a whole.

How do managers design resource delivery systems? The following guidelines have proved helpful:

1. List all resources which could help (assume you have a magic wand to command what you wish).
2. Draw the ideal resource requirements as a concept diagram (with arrows, flows, interrelationships etc.).
3. Ask 'What is possible?' (Try to obtain or develop as many resources as you can.)
4. Define critical resources (those that will cause failure or deterioration if they are absent or defective).
5. Set time lines (decide when you require resources to be on stream).
6. Devise a resource utilization plan (set criteria to judge the effectiveness of each element).
7. Develop a budget (so that costs are transparent).

CONTINUOUS IMPROVEMENT

In recent years the Japanese word 'kaizen' has become well known in progressive organizations around the world. Loosely translated kaizen means 'continuous improvement'; it has become an extremely powerful management tool of special interest to first-level managers. The key principles of continuous improvement are:

❑ Everything can be improved.
❑ Quality is achieved through a myriad of incremental but small improvements.
❑ The people doing the job often produce the best ideas.
❑ Empowered people will generate change for themselves.

The principle of continuous improvement can be enlarged and developed into a set of concepts called 'the learning organization'. This approach begins with the recognition that nothing is static; knowledge is the pre-eminent source of competitive advantage and learning needs to be pursued at individual, group and organizational levels.

Any organizational form may be defective. The act of organizing generates both strengths and weaknesses. Consider, for example, an international firm that moves from an organization based on product lines to one that is geographically based. There are advantages, for example, a flexible focus on markets and clear ownership of sales, but the disadvantages may be that product development is weakened and a fragmented approach to R & D undermines effectiveness.

The essence of continuous incremental improvement is not major transformation. Each time an activity is undertaken there is an opportunity for improvement. This rarely occurs naturally – a conscious critique needs to be undertaken to identify specific learning points. The following suggestions should ensure continuous improvement:

- ❑ Communicate the benefits of continuous improvement.
- ❑ Train managers in the skills of problem finding and problem solving.
- ❑ Review all activities or sample activities.
- ❑ Use the creativity and experience of those directly involved.
- ❑ Come to definite conclusions from each meeting.
- ❑ Implement changes so that the 'can do' ethos is developed.

THE MANAGER ROLE – ORGANIZING PEOPLE AND RESOURCES

Every manager is a 'supervisor'. His or her job involves the direction, control and coordination of resources.

THE MANAGER AS ORGANIZER

The word 'supervisor' implies 'superior vision'. The supervisor (we are using this term in the American sense of 'the boss') is subject to many pressures. The role must be clarified from the start.

Supervisors can help themselves by systematically analysing the pressures they are under and the conflicts that arise. In our experience, this is best undertaken by discussion groups from the same organization. Use the following list of pressures and questions relevant to every supervisor:

Pressures	*Questions*
Expectations of boss	How is my performance measured?
	What are my objectives?

Economic forces	What effects do economic forces bring to bear? What changes need to happen?
Company systems	How much time is taken up with procedures? What are the limits to my autonomy?
Reward systems	What behaviour is rewarded? What behaviour is punished?
Expectations of colleagues	What do I have to do to fit in? What 'professional' standards are expected of me?
Training procedures	Is learning adequately managed? What attitudes are inculcated by training? How can I facilitate learning in my section?
Expectations of work people	How do they expect me to behave? What is their response to discipline? How well will they work without me?
Trade union power	Do I give and receive adequate communication? Is my influence undermined by unions?
Age and ambitions	What are my own expectations from my working life? What is important to me? How much am I prepared to change for job development?
Technology requirements	What special demands does technology make?

There are many other forces that pull a supervisor in one direction or another, and they often conflict. A supervisor must disentangle numerous pressures and sometimes the choices are difficult. Therefore, the most important supervisory skill is to be able to cope creatively with permanently difficult situations. This requires resilience and the ability to avoid that state of world-weary resignation that afflicts many of those who have been battered by constant change. Despite difficulties, the supervisor needs to:

- ❑ Make choices without clear guidelines.
- ❑ Channel and exploit resources.
- ❑ Develop procedures to coordinate effort.
- ❑ Plan and initiate change.
- ❑ Develop resilience and the capacity for long-term effectiveness.

Defining the supervisory role can easily become an exercise in meaningless generalities that combine platitudes with empty managerial jargon. The most useful process for supervisors is to review their current experiences with others who face similar problems. It is probable that some supervisors react defensively and blame their problems on others rather than take personal responsibility for them. When the flood of resentment has been discharged, it is possible to examine available options. From this assessment, a personal definition of role can be expressed in down-to-earth and specific language.

THE 'NEW PARADIGM'

The role of the supervisor has changed dramatically in the last decades of the twentieth century. The scale and scope of the changes are best understood by a comparative table (the words are simplistic but the meaning is profound) – see Table 2.

All jobs are essentially concerned with transforming *inputs* into *outputs*. This idea can be shown as in Figure 9.

This figure leads to four questions:
1. What outputs are required from the job?
2. What is the most effective way to transform inputs?
3. What inputs are needed to make the process happen?
4. How can effective feedback be provided?

Table 2 The role of the supervisor

'Old' supervisory role	'New' supervisory role
Controller	Leader
Reporter (up the hierarchy)	Empowerer
Disciplinarian	Role model
Decision maker	Guide
Problem solver	Enabler
Instructor	Coach
Planner	Coordinator
Standard setter	Reviewer
'Boss'	'Facilitator'

In almost all businesses where people work together, one person's outputs become another person's inputs. Most managers and supervisors tend to concentrate on outputs because, understandably, they are interested in results. On the other hand, those being managed tend to dwell on the inputs. Typically, they feel dependent on other links in the chain and grumble about the inefficiency of other departments. The systems approach enables us to examine the issue at six levels and each level is broader than the previous one.

1. *Tasks*   Those distinct, time-consuming activities that take your energy.
2. *Job*   The whole of your activities and contributions.
3. *Team*   The work of the function, department, gang, or area.
4. *Process*   Flows of activities that cross departmental boundaries.
5. *Department/site*   A whole function, or a distinct operating unit combining several teams.
6. *Organization*   The enterprise as a whole.

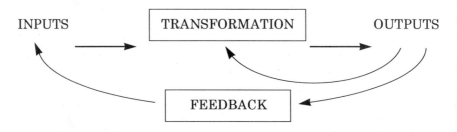

Figure 9 Transforming inputs into outputs

It makes sense to review systematically those levels that you can personally influence.

SHARING RESPONSIBILITY

One of the most important principles in the 'new paradigm' of management is sharing responsibility. Do not listen to those who say that responsibility cannot be shared. It happens!

Almost every organization gives managers and supervisors responsibility for a wider range of tasks than they can possibly handle alone. Others are needed to help them fulfil their responsibilities. This calls for *delegation* – passing responsibility downward. However, many managers find it difficult to delegate. They fear the important aspects of the job will be neglected or bungled, so they are tempted to undertake such tasks themselves. Some of the advantages and disadvantages of delegation are as follows:

Advantages	*Disadvantages*
Less strain	Quality may suffer
Greater capacity for team success	Work may not be completed
Better development of subordinates	Communication is more complex
Faster response time	Strong individuals may pose a threat to the manager
More energetic teamwork	Decision making is more complex
Greater creativity	Manager is less stimulated

Despite the possible pitfalls, the case for delegation is overwhelming, and successful managers are those who can delegate competently. Delegation comprises a set of skills that can be developed, as follows:

Consider the risks

Effective delegation means that the inherent risks are seen, weighed and minimized. You can do this by stretching but not breaking subordinates and by developing your own skills in managing delegation.

Delegate to able people

Delegation is useful both to the organization and to the individual who is ready for more responsibility. When people do not have the capacity or the will to undertake new assignments the skilful manager should coach them on improving their job performance.

Pace your delegation

Expanding individual capacity takes time and the skilful manager will pace the increase of responsibility appropriately.

Excessive demands result in personal stress, patchy performance, doubtful quality and a risk of failure, but insufficient demand is wasteful and demoralizing.

Agree on clear objectives

Skilful delegation requires clearly established and mutually accepted objectives and specific criteria for success. If objectives are not set, then the task remains unclear, freedom of action is restricted and it is impossible to assess performance.

Monitor progress

Try to come to a shared understanding of what 'progress' means and how it can be assessed objectively. Establishing procedures for monitoring gives a sense of security, reduces risk and provides a basis for counselling.

Regular counselling

Delegation is a form of management development, and assignments can be used as opportunities for developing others. A systematic process of coaching helps both parties because the subordinate being coached receives guidance in how to perform the task, while the manager gains more peace of mind. Coaching requires more time than a five-minute chat over a cup of coffee. There should be enough time for an in-depth examination of the process being used to work on the task or assignment.

Look for delegation opportunities

Every manager delegates, and the skilful manager will seek opportunities to increase delegation. However, delegating excessively will provoke resentment and indicate that the management role is being neglected.

Understand the limits of authority

A manager can only delegate assigned authority, so that the limits of that authority must be clearly understood.

This is an exciting time to be a manager. Horizons have broadened to the extent that standards are set by the international community (this is why we use the term 'world-class'). Principles of organization have been turned on their heads so that many of the absolute certainties enshrined in dusty management textbooks are now recognized to be negative, limiting and wrong. To illustrate the point, here are a few of the changes in managerial thinking:

❏   Rigid hierarchy used to be the architecture of the corporation and is now a flexible structure on which to build networks.

❏   Functions used to be islands of specialization and are now pools of expertise.

❏   Bosses used to control; now they enable.

❑ Organizations were conceptualized as machines; now they are seen as systems, flows of energy or representations of a chaotic universe.
❑ Control used to be sucked to the centre; now it is shared widely.
❑ Strategy used to be a long-term plan; now it is a dynamic process of moving towards an intent by incremental or unplannable steps.

These changes in the nature of organization and, therefore, the task of organizing will stretch us all. But there is no alternative: managers will need to transform their mind-sets to comprehend this new definition of their role.

 CHARACTERISTICS OF MANAGERS WITH GOOD/POOR ORGANIZING SKILLS

The characteristics of those with poor/good organizing skills are shown in the following.

Poor organizing skills	*Good organizing skills*
Defines tasks as isolated elements	Sees 'the big picture'
Fails to break down 'big' tasks	'Chunks' big tasks into manageable elements
Does not develop capability	Develops organizational capability
Does not balance resources for task achievement	Balances resources to avoid 'weak links'
Does not practise continuous improvement	Practises continuous improvement
Is not clear of role requirements	Is clear about role requirements
Controls others	Leads others
Confines others	Empowers others
Limits others	Coaches others
Centralizes power in his/her own hands	Delegates and engages others
Compartmentalized thinking guides action	Works easily across boundaries
Thinks of the organization as a machine	Thinks of the organization as a combination of organization and system

WHEN MANAGERS MOST NEED ORGANIZING SKILLS

Organizing is one of the main elements of the manager's role, common to all managerial and supervisory jobs. The requirement is least developed in those jobs where behaviour is predefined (like being the shift manager in a McDonald's outlet). Managers who lead projects, deal with complex or volatile situations or handle pools of resources are most in need of these skills.

BLOCKAGE

10

WEAK TEAMBUILDING CAPACITY

The atmosphere in the meeting was tense and heavy. The senior management team had received a shock. Their division had been expected to make a handsome profit, but a recent audit had revealed that basic flaws in costing would result in a substantial loss instead.

The divisional chief executive was ashen-faced as he said, 'When I was at headquarters, the chairman said, "You've just used up eight of your nine lives! Our position couldn't be worse. I feel that I'd like to hang, draw and quarter the culprit, but let's analyse the problem. Where did we go wrong?"'

The group was silent until one manager responded, 'Well, the problem is that no one is specifically responsible for relating cost projections to market forecasts. We operate functionally, and the only person with an overall view is you as chief executive. You are the hub; we all feed information in to you and you are the only one who can make overall decisions.' The other managers nodded in agreement with this analysis of their managerial process.

Then the chief executive said, 'You can't expect me to understand all that detail. It's your job to make the processes work and you must have been aware that something was wrong.'

There was a pause before a man cleared his throat nervously and said, 'I think that several of us are wary of highlighting problems because experience suggests that we are likely to be in deep trouble if we speak up.'

The chief executive replied, 'It is now clear to me that there needs to be much more frankness and openness in our relations with one another. How are we going to improve matters?'

One of the managers replied, 'I think the problem is that we don't operate as a team. We are all so busy protecting our own territories that problems we share simply aren't tackled. We need to operate as one unit rather than as a collection of individuals.'

As organizations and tasks become more complex, managers have to develop the effectiveness of their groups to achieve coordinated results and sustain high morale. In recent years, we have clearly diagnosed the characteristics of effective working groups and learned to express them in down-to-earth terms. Today's manager needs teambuilding skills in order to sustain groups that consistently achieve good results.

Teambuilding skills can be categorized under four headings:
1.   Recognizing the potential of teambuilding
2.   The role of the team leader
3.   Developing team maturity
4.   Overcoming blockages to effective teamwork.

We have published detailed descriptions and activities for teambuilding elsewhere,[1] and the ideas outlined in this chapter are described in greater depth in those books. This chapter presents basic ideas on how to become a more effective team manager.

 ## RECOGNIZING THE POTENTIAL OF TEAMBUILDING

A team can accomplish much more than the sum of its individual members. However, groups often fail to achieve even a small fraction of their potential. It is a common experience for group interactions to be lifeless, defensive, unsatisfying, confusing and ineffective. This is a costly defect in any organization because effective management requires that people come together to coordinate resources, clarify objectives, initiate and sponsor ideas, plan operations and accomplish tasks despite obstacles.

Some managers have little belief in the value of a team approach. Perhaps they have sat through too many tedious meetings in which the pace of decision making slowed to a snail's pace when contributions were invited from the group, or the manager feels that he or she is burdened by the requirement to take others along and it is easier to do it yourself! We believe the opposite. The team has been accurately described as 'the most powerful tool known to man'. It can be uniquely stimulating, supportive and energetic. Individuals enjoy being part of a team, commit themselves to it, set high standards and create a stimulating and creative environment. Managers undertake teambuilding for several reasons:

❑   A team approach is an affirmative management style.
❑   Stress is reduced as problems are shared.
❑   Teams are the best way to manage coordination.
❑   More ideas are generated, so the capacity to innovate is increased.

[1.] D. Francis and D. Young, *Improving Work Groups: A practical manual for team building* (2nd ed.), San Diego, CA: University Associates, 1994; Mike Woodcock, *Team Development Manual* (2nd ed.), Gower, 1989; Mike Woodcock, *50 Activities for Teambuilding*, Gower, 1993.

❑   Large or interdisciplinary issues are better resolved by using a team approach.
❑   Interpersonal difficulties, confusion over roles and poor personal contributions can often be resolved successfully in a team.
❑   Being a member of a team is nurturing and motivating.

The team approach is not a panacea for all management problems but it can help people who need to work with each other to achieve shared objectives quickly, efficiently and enjoyably. Teamwork requires every member to strive to make the team a success. All team members must deliberately 'opt in'. There is no place for 'scoring points' and gaining personal advantage.

A team shares common tasks that require combined efforts. It is not easy to create a team. Effective teams have to be constructed methodically and painstakingly. Relationships have to be built, sometimes painful issues must be exposed and resolved, work methods improved and an energetic and positive climate created. The group has a life of its own; one of the distinctive features of a team is its strong sense of identity.

THE ROLE OF THE TEAM LEADER

The leader plays a unique and crucial role in the development of the team. Team members invariably watch their leader's management style and react to his or her ability to promote openness, cooperation and team effectiveness. A manager may announce an intention to adopt team management principles but then behave in ways that clearly demonstrate a lack of commitment to the team approach to management. Without effort, personal integrity and trust, a team cannot be developed.

ESTABLISHING TEAMBUILDING PRIORITIES

When a manager is deciding whether to use a team approach, the initial step should be to assess whether it is worth the cost and effort required.[1] Each group should be examined to determine whether it is receptive and significant. The following indicates which groups are most likely to benefit from team effectiveness:

Priority for team effectiveness	*Team character*
Very high priority	Team members are highly interdependent and are collectively responsible for achieving large-scale objectives that have a significant effect on the organization's profitability or effectiveness. Team members must work well together to achieve results. Survival of the organization would be jeopardized by failure.
High priority	Team members are interdependent and need to be effective and competent to perform. The team makes a significant contribution to organizational effectiveness. Poor performance would lead to unresolved problems, wasted opportunities or low morale.
Medium priority	This team has clear objectives but can achieve success without high levels of interdependence. Team members have distinct roles with individual responsibilities and each contributes to the team as an 'expert' or 'specialist'.
Low priority	A group exists but its performance as a team has only a minor impact on the success of the enterprise. However, team development would benefit morale and motivation.

---

[1] See Mike Woodcock and Dave Francis, *Teambuilding Strategy*, Gower, 1994.

Very low priority

This group lacks a shared objective and is relatively unimportant in the organization. Capability has little relationship to team effectiveness because individual performance is the key factor.

 ## TEAM LEADERSHIP

Emotion and commitment are the main ingredients in effective teamwork. As one manager said: 'Being a team means that when you get a request from another team member your immediate reaction is "Yes, I can provide this and can I do anything else to help?" not "Hell, here's another job: how can I do it with the minimum effort?" Also it means thinking "That worked well, I'll share it with others", not 'That worked well: it will give me more status".'

The emotional element in teamwork is not easy to create. Simply wishing that people cared for each other is insufficient. Ways must be found to allow people to get to know each other, be touched by each other's feelings, develop a sense of mutual commitment and behave with the intention of helping others. Such an attitude cannot be manufactured but it is a natural human response (we are pack animals) and so it can be facilitated.

Of particular significance is behaviour in times of stress or tension. If warmth is replaced by punishment, people will either cower or fight but both reactions diminish the team's strength. As a team develops members learn to accept each other's 'weaknesses' with compassion. Negative initial behaviour may be sufficient to prevent an authentic relationship from developing. As the team evolves so members come to accept that all their colleagues have flaws (this includes themselves).

It is an important step in the evolution of a team when 'weaknesses' can be shared and accepted. Ironically, the recognition of inadequacy is a prelude to achieving collective strength. The openness needed evolves hand-in-hand with trust. It takes a person who is unusually secure, bold or foolish to be open without trust. Since trust is based on believing the other person is on your side (not indifferent or against you), personal weaknesses are shared increasingly as trust develops.

The team leader plays an important role in facilitating an open, trusting climate. We can model openness and humanness and not be weakened by recognitions of imperfection – this gives permission for other team members to expose their true feelings to each other. The process proceeds one step at a time. Honesty evolves layer by layer. At each step team members are taking a risk – so if disclosure is treated disrespectfully then the sense of betrayal may be impossible to forget.

THE TEAMBUILDER'S CHARTER

Once a firm commitment to use a team approach has been made the group undertakes a teambuilding process. Sometimes this is formally structured by especially designed team workshops. Often the teambuilding process is informal but every team needs to undertake this process in its own way. We have found that competent teambuilders often share a similar approach, summarized here:

Establish shared aims	Groups can often find their own way if they know where to go. Without shared aims people do not see why they should 'opt in'.
Proceed step by step	Success builds both confidence and further success. Big tasks have to be tackled chunk by chunk.
Avoid excessive complexity	People are more comfortable with concepts they can grasp. Too complex tasks are avoided.
Ensure agreement before commitment	Commitment grows from real understanding. Change without commitment is almost impossible. Gaining commitment is time-consuming.

Build realistic timetables	'Rome was not built in a day.' Unlearning often needs to precede learning.
Be participative	All team members have valuable contributions to make. Consultation increases commitment. Consultation is not a chore; it is an essential. Domination by the boss undermines teambuilding.
Relate teambuilding to organizational work	Initiatives are more likely to be accepted if they are organizationally relevant. Use regular meetings or projects as teambuilding opportunities. Ensure the reward structure supports teamwork.
Face up to interpersonal difficulties	Do not sweep issues under the carpet. Be realistic about what is attainable. Playing politics will discredit your efforts. Create a culture in which it is OK to share 'weaknesses'.
Encourage openness and frankness	Decisions are improved when issues are discussed openly. Do not stifle discussion. Allow emotions to be aired. Encourage potential problems to be surfaced.
Do not raise false expectations	Promises are easy. Broken promises discredit.
Reorganize work if necessary	Developmental activities take time. Teambuilding can increase individual work loads.

Remember that the unknown is often more threatening than the known	When problems are exposed, they become less threatening. Sharing problems and difficulties gives support.
Remember that development is basically self-regulated	Age, capacity and beliefs create limitations – accept the 'rough edges' in others. Ultimately, we are responsible for our own development.
Remember that 'You can lead a horse to water, but you cannot make it drink'	People cannot be forced into attitude changes. People cannot be forced into openness and honesty. People can be forced into pretending to change. Being a member of a team is a personal decision.
Remember those who are not part of the action	Jealousy can develop. People like to be part of the action. Strengthening one team can weaken others.
Remember that team building can precipitate other problems	Individuals and teams can grow beyond their present roles. Latent difficulties become public.
Be open to other opportunities when team building	Individual development can occur. New ideas generate further creativity. Challenges to existing systems and methods may present themselves.
Accept external help if necessary	Choose carefully. Take responsibility for your own actions. Outsiders offer different insights and skills.

	Outsiders do not have organizational histories.
	Outsiders are more likely to be impartial.
Learn from mistakes	Admit when you are wrong.
	Review progress regularly.
	Encourage feedback.
	Honest feedback is the most valuable thing your colleagues can give you.
Build linkages	Build relationships with linked teams.
	Focus on internal and external customers.
Practise what you preach	'Actions speak louder than words.'

 ## TEAM LEADERSHIP

The team leader must be aware of the needs of the group and have sufficient understanding of the concept of teambuilding to steer the group through a series of developmental stages. An open approach is vital. All issues affecting the group must be talked through, feedback given and received and time spent clarifying expectations. The team leader must demonstrate the high level of openness needed for a team approach and be watchful of team members, identifying their individual needs and enabling each to be developed and strengthened as the team matures. Follow these guidelines:

- ❑ All team members are clear about the objectives of the team.
- ❑ Individual skills are identified and roles clarified.
- ❑ The team is structured appropriately for the needs of the task.
- ❑ Diversity is prized, not derided.
- ❑ The team reflects on its work methods and sets targets for improvement.
- ❑ The team develops a self-discipline that uses time and resources well.

❑   The team has sufficient opportunities to meet and work through any problems.
❑   The team supports members and develops close relationships.
❑   The team has open relationships and is prepared to confront difficulties and blockages to effectiveness.

 ## TRUST

Team managers must commit themselves to relating with others directly and honestly. Few roles in society expose the integrity of an individual as extensively as management. Team managers who use their power for manipulation, demoralizing others, or restricting potential are soon detected, scorned and mistrusted. Trust grows under three conditions: first, people tell the truth; second, they are consistent, and third, people feel that the other person is on their side. Trust is a prerequisite for the development of a healthy and productive team. It is built up by people saying what they mean and eliminating areas of uncertainty or operational weakness. Although techniques of leadership may be taught, each individual needs to clarify and express an approach that is strictly personal and consistent with held values. Team leaders who are mature and effective have developed a deep-rooted personal approach, appropriate to the task, that is warm, open, direct and problem-solving and sets high standards for others and self.

 ## DEVELOPING TEAM MATURITY – STAGES

Teams possess their own character, like people, and it is impossible to predict accurately how they will behave, but as teams develop they tend to go through six stages that build on past development. The following pattern is often visible.

STAGE ONE: RITUAL SNIFFING

The new team may look businesslike and organized on the surface, but underneath people are watching each other to determine how far they wish to become involved. Feelings are often hidden, one individual controls with authority, and cooperation follows an established ritual. Little fundamental questioning of objectives and work methods takes place. Often people do not care for others, listening is poor, and creative, energetic teamwork is virtually absent.

STAGE TWO: INFIGHTING

Many teams go through a period of upheaval. Conflicts are more significant than cooperation. The contribution of the team leader is critically evaluated, alliances and cliques are formed and differences are expressed negatively. Relationships become significant and personal strengths or weaknesses are exposed. The team begins to explore the issue of commitment and to experiment with ways of improving relationships. Sometimes there is a power struggle over leadership or between strong individuals in the group. Little satisfaction is expressed by members.

STAGE THREE: EXPERIMENTATION

If the team works through the infighting stage it faces the problem of how to use the talent and resources now available. Often the team is working in a fragmented and unstructured way. However, there is energy and interest in learning how to function better. Operating methods are reviewed, there is a willingness to experiment, and activities to improve performance are undertaken. More risky issues are opened up and less vocal members begin to contribute.

STAGE FOUR: EFFECTIVENESS

The team is becoming skilful at tackling problems and using resources successfully. Emphasis is placed on making good use of time and clarifying objectives. Many issues must be worked through, including mission, values, roles, policies, resource allocation, leadership, cooperation and interfaces with other parts of the organization. Pride develops in being a member of a 'winning' team. Problems are faced realistically and solved creatively. Leadership functions may be exercised flexibly by different members of the team, depending on the task in hand.

STAGE FIVE: MATURITY

A mature team has developed close bonds among its members. Members are accepted and valued for what they are, rather than for how they wish to appear. Relationships are informal and satisfying. Personal disagreements are rapidly resolved. The team has become a successful social unit and is admired from without. It is capable of superb performance and sets high standards of achievement.

STAGE SIX: DEGENERATION

Teams that have operated together for a long time begin to decline, processes become mechanical, 'group think' confines thinking and ideas dry up. It is time for regeneration.

The process is shown in Table 3.

The effective team leader helps the group to progress through the development stages to maturity. Initially, he/she will clarify objectives, suggest procedures, set standards and encourage people to get to know each other. Sometimes, this may require an assertive and authoritarian approach. Further development of the team involves

Table 3 Stages of team development

Testing out Feelings kept hidden Conforming to established line Apprehensive of change Authority central Little listening Little care for others Personal weaknesses covered up Mistakes used as evidence Objectives poorly set Objectives poorly communicated	Stage 1 Ritual sniffing
Team leader performance evaluated Relationships more significant Alliances and cliques formed Personal strengths/weaknesses known Commitment debated Interest in climate Team needs come to the fore Differences expressed more openly	Stage 2 Infighting

Members protect team Not working in unified way Not working in methodical way More dynamic and exciting functioning Dormant people begin to contribute Review of operating methods Performance improvement activities undertaken Willingness to experiment Values and assumptions debated Risky issues opened up Leadership or management discussed Personal animosities dealt with Inward-looking Better listening		Stage 3 Experimentation
Operating methods examined Procedures reviewed Problem-solving skills developed Frequent review Clear objectives Search for economy Problems handled creatively Team pride		Stage 4 Effectiveness
Openness, concern and improved relationships of Stage 3 PLUS Effective working methods of Stage 4	Informality and respect Success emulated by others Happy and rewarding Outside help welcomed Open relationships with other groups	Stage 5 Maturity
Insular thinking Low energy Complacency Absence of creative conflict Orthodox thinking Superiority syndrome Lack of outward challenge Tiredness shows 'Group think' sets in Unrealistic, insular and irrational decision making Divergence not tolerated		Stage 6 Degeneration

creating opportunities to meet, developing an open climate, ensuring that comprehensive review takes place and preparing to share information and parts of the decision-making process.

The team leader must also be able to predict the next phase of team development and steer the group toward the opportunities and problems ahead. As the quality of teamwork improves, so do the possibilities for innovation in leadership processes. Different tasks may be led by different individuals whose roles change according to their skills. Increasingly, tasks are delegated and there is a wider involvement in planning and decision making. The team leader helps steer the group through the stages of growth and, both by example and by leadership, helps the team progress towards its full potential. He or she is also watchful for any signs of degeneration. When this happens a 'shake-up' is needed to bring new energy and rekindle openness.

OVERCOMING BLOCKAGES TO EFFECTIVE TEAMWORK

During the journey from group immaturity to being a mature and effective team, the group may find from time to time that it fails to make progress. A key symptom of a blocked team is low energy and poor performance. Blockages need to be identified because, once they are understood, team problems are easier to resolve. We have identified ten blocks that frequently occur in teams.

BLOCKAGE 1: INAPPROPRIATE LEADERSHIP

Leadership is perhaps the most important factor in determining the quality of teamwork. A leader who is unwilling to use a team approach, or who lacks the skills to develop this style of management, will squash any initiative to build a team.

The effective leader will emphasize, and show by example, that issues are worked through to clear resolution. The following characteristics of success frequently stand out. The effective team leader:

❑   is true to personal beliefs and is considered by others to have integrity;

❏ uses delegation to increase participation and power sharing;
❏ is clear about standards;
❏ is willing and able to give and receive trust and loyalty;
❏ has the personal strength to maintain the integrity and position of the team;
❏ is receptive to the hopes, fears and needs of others and respects their dignity;
❏ is prepared to examine his/her role;
❏ faces facts honestly;
❏ encourages personal and team development;
❏ establishes and maintains effective working practices;
❏ tries to make work a happy, exciting and rewarding place.

BLOCKAGE 2: UNQUALIFIED MEMBERSHIP

A team is more than the sum of individual talents. A team needs a balanced membership of people who can work together. Various roles need to be filled in any team, and an analysis of these provides a basis for the construction of a balanced and vibrant group. For example, a team may need an 'ideas' person, an 'analyst', a 'driving force', a 'planner', a 'restraining factor', and several 'doers'. It is possible that each member contributes one or more of these necessary roles. When a crucial contribution is missing, the team must generate it.

If team members lack basic skills, the team may be incapable of making a high-level contribution. A team needs a balance of technical skills and personal attributes that, when taken together, give it the capability to tackle jobs effectively.

BLOCKAGE 3: UNCONSTRUCTIVE CLIMATE

The people who join a team may be from diverse backgrounds with a wide range of values and expectations. A team approach needs an affirmative climate that bridges differences.

One test of a positive climate is whether people feel committed to the objectives of the group. Commitment to a team develops over time and only emerges when individuals have made personal decisions to devote their energy to the objectives of the group. The growth of commitment is one index of team maturity. As their emotional bonds develop, team members become more prepared to serve common goals actively and a great deal of satisfaction is derived from participation. The group develops a warmth that combines directness and honesty with concern for the welfare of members.

BLOCKAGE 4: UNCLEAR OBJECTIVES

The first step in achievement is clarifying what you want to achieve. An able and mature team can achieve goals once members are clear on the desired outcome. Team members are more likely to be committed to objectives if they have been involved in their clarification and feel a sense of ownership of them. This agreement can be difficult to reach, but experience tells us that it is a prerequisite of an effective team and well worth the trouble.

If a team lacks a clear view of what it is to achieve, then it follows that individual members cannot contribute toward its success. Even when team objectives are understood, it is important to bridge the gap between personal and group needs. An effective team enables each individual to meet personal objectives and contribute to the achievement of team objectives. Useful objectives for a team usually meet the following criteria:

❏ Objectives are defined after debate.
❏ There are 'owners' for each objective.
❏ Objectives are adopted after all stakeholders' interests have been assessed.
❏ A strong emphasis is placed on results to be achieved rather than on things to do.
❏ Objectives are stated in ways that clearly identify the results required, methods of measurement, and a timetable for review.
❏ Objectives are felt to be achievable with the resources available.
❏ Objectives do not pull the team in different directions at once.

Team and individual objectives need to be changed over time. The team that looks ahead, foresees difficulties, seizes opportunities, and redefines its aims in the light of experience will ultimately succeed.

BLOCKAGE 5: LOW STANDARDS

Sometimes teams lack basic standards: they are not world-class. The purpose of a work group is to achieve tangible results that meet the needs of the organization. When a team meets its members' needs for social contact but fails to perform, it is failing a critical test.

Standards have several dimensions. These are the most significant:

1. Standards must meet customer needs and expectations.
2. They must ensure cost efficiency and economy of effort.
3. They must enable consistency to be assured.
4. They must stretch individuals so that human assets are not wasted.

An effective team sets high standards of achievement that greatly affect how the team operates. Achievement should be recognized and rewarded within the team. Rewards need not be financial, as many people feel that personal recognition is as significant as cash in hand. For members, some of the most satisfying teams are those that achieve results well above average. For example, soldiers in élite regiments are more positive than those in 'ordinary' regiments. The pursuit of excellence, even in everyday or mundane activities, is a great motivator. It stimulates individual competence, fosters pride and increases each person's sense of worth.

BLOCKAGE 6: INEFFECTIVE WORK METHODS

Sound working methods and effective decision-making procedures are essential to any work team. Issues to consider include:

- ❑ Mission and vision
- ❑ Ways in which decisions are taken
- ❑ Collection and display of information
- ❑ Communication within and outside the team
- ❑ Whether resources are effectively coordinated
- ❑ Procedures for reviewing decisions
- ❑ Planning processes
- ❑ Criteria to measure effectiveness.

The effective team has honed its working methods to become an informal but strong discipline. The group learns that it can apply standards of quality to its meetings. Individual members have developed personal skills that are appreciated and utilized by the team. There is an air of competence, and boredom is rarely felt at meetings. The team quickly moves forward and maintains a rapid pace but a high level of personal attention and economy of expression ensure that relevant issues are explored.

BLOCKAGE 7: INSUFFICIENT OPENNESS AND CONFRONTATION

Some teams operate an informal conspiracy by refusing to review people and events in an analytical and critical way. Such teams inhibit the free flow of judgement and comment, preferring a polite but suppressed climate. Withholding by team members exists for several reasons:

- ❑ *Politeness* Team members may feel that social etiquette precludes confrontation.

❑   *Fear of loss of face* Individuals may see criticism as an unwelcome whittling away of their self-images.

❑   *Refusal to 'rock the boat'* Team members may consider criticism to be a means of exposing weakness and undermining morale.

❑   *Inadequate skills* Team members appreciate the benefits of intensive review, but simply do not feel able to handle it constructively; they lack the skills of analysis and personal confrontation required.

❑   *Fear* If a person feels vulnerable he/she is far less likely to contribute.

'Post mortems' of both specific projects and routine working are useful. These reviews are the learning material for the team. We call this aspect of team work the 'critique'. Individuals gather to analyse the strengths and weaknesses of their performance, are open about their personal assessments, and can take negative comments without rancour.

If a team is to be successful, its members must be able to state their views about each other and air differences and problems without fear of ridicule or retaliation. If team members are unwilling to express themselves, much energy, effort and creativity are lost. Effective teams do not avoid delicate or unpleasant issues, but confront them honestly and squarely.

The management of confrontation is never easy. No matter how much care is taken feelings can be badly bruised. We learn from Asian cultures the importance of confronting issues rather than people, and the need to provide dignity to those who are proved wrong. Confrontation, properly managed and constructively employed, leads to a greater understanding among team members. Positive conflict results in openness, reduced tension, better relationships and greater trust. Negative conflict breeds mistrust and hostility.

BLOCKAGE 8: UNDEVELOPED INDIVIDUALS

Teams pool the skills of individuals. It follows that the most capable teams are those with at least some members of outstanding individual ability. Ability may be unrelated to education, qualifications or experience. Many managers seem to possess all the appropriate skills and knowledge but have never achieved worthwhile results. Others have received little training and seem, on the surface, to be deficient in management skills but they have created immensely successful businesses.

The team is a vehicle for individual development. When members join a team, they should be introduced with understanding and with firmness. The team has to make demands and the individual must not be made to feel that 'coasting' is acceptable. Every member needs to feel that belonging is a privilege. We define strongly developed team members as those who:

❑   have world-class technical talent;
❑   have energy;
❑   are in touch with their feelings;
❑   are prepared to be open;
❑   will change a viewpoint through reason but not dominance;
❑   put their viewpoints well.

Observers have noted that strongly developed team members display personal characteristics that are different from those of their less effective colleagues. People who tend to achieve little as individuals seem to adopt a passive approach to life, seeking to retreat to stability. They find challenge frightening and avoid it whenever possible. They do not seek insight into themselves and their beliefs, and feedback and criticism are seen as unhelpful and threatening. For them, life would be happier if they were surrounded by weak people, but they are not, and they often resent others they see making a success of difficult situations.

In contrast, people who often achieve good results seem to take an active approach to life. They make things happen and seek new challenges. They wish to know more about themselves and are interested in the feedback that others can give them. They welcome constructive criticism, recognize that time and energy are finite and so try to make the best use of their valuable resources. Individuals who are strongly developed are better resources for themselves and add to the power of the team.

BLOCKAGE 9: LOW INNOVATIVE CAPACITY

Effective teams can generate creative ideas and put them into practice. Consider for a few moments the innovation process. First, a need has to be identified – the 'missing link' must be perceived. Then a new idea is needed. This can be a logical extension of an existing stream of thought or a radical departure from it. The idea is seldom clear or fully worked out at its inception. It must be developed, enlarged, extended and simplified, then tested. (Ideas must work or they are merely topics for academic debate.) This process is often aided by a special kind of teamwork. Innovative capacity can be usefully divided into the following five steps:

1. Identifying a need – the 'missing link'.
2. Generating germs of ideas.
3. Developing mature proposals.
4. Testing proposals.
5. Applying the new idea.

Much depends on a hard-to-define corporate attitude toward innovation. Some organizations have managed to become exciting places in which to work, and this generates much vitality. One experienced manager says that a key task of management is to realize the 'latent energy' available in the workforce, by using both incremental continuous improvement (CI) and large-scale change processes (transformation). The bored repetition of meaningless tasks increases frustration and depresses vitality, enthusiasm and innovation. From the viewpoint of organizational health, this is dangerous because it deprives the system of creative potential and increases resistance to change.

Harnessing creativity requires more than an openness to innovate. Skills and procedures that can help are clearly identifiable, yet the most highly trained and experienced creative people continue to make errors because risk cannot be eliminated. Accordingly, a willingness to accept failure and learn from it is needed.

BLOCKAGE 10: UNCONSTRUCTIVE INTERTEAM RELATIONSHIPS

Teams usually interrelate with other groups, but often the quality of cooperation is poor. Unsatisfactory communication and lack of shared objectives are often present.

Managers frequently talk about their jobs in terms borrowed from sports. They speak of 'playing to win', 'scoring points', and 'the name of the game'. Such expressions signal how people think about their jobs and what mental pictures help them to interpret what happens. The team leader has a special role to play in improving interteam relationships and can do much to prevent hostility and to build cooperation. The management of interteam relationships is a crucial element in organizational effectiveness. In recent years we have recognized the weaknesses in functional organizations which promote a compartmentalized mentality and fail to develop the notion of the organization as a network of customer–supplier relationships. By taking the following steps, the team leader can help to build positive interteam relationships:

❑ Map processes which overlap teams.
❑ Identify common objectives.

❑   Develop personal understanding.
❑   Provide opportunities for regular problem solving.
❑   Build a climate of trust.
❑   Establish a management structure to supervise cross-department teamwork.

Skills of teambuilding became significant in the second half of the twentieth century. They will be even more so in the twenty-first. As organizations shrink to a core staff with frequent free-flowing associations on a project basis, old forms of command and control will need to be replaced by more organic organizational models.

Teams are the building blocks of the organization of tomorrow. However, the team will take on many guises. Sometimes it will be a formal group with identified membership. More frequently there will be *ad hoc* groups established for short-term projects. Even more interesting will be groups that have no immediate physical connection but work together as a 'virtual' team inside computer systems. Teamwork is the core competence in organizations which evolve like a biological system using shared knowledge as the crucial resource. The skills described in this chapter are exciting and important – and necessary for all managers.

 ## CHARACTERISTICS OF MANAGERS WITH STRONG/WEAK TEAMBUILDING CAPACITY

Teambuilding is a positive management tool because it generates a high-energy group that is resourceful, effective and responsive. Managers and supervisors who are competent at teambuilding have the characteristics listed here on the right-hand side. Those who fail to develop a team approach display the characteristics listed on the left.

Weak teambuilding capacity	*Strong teambuilding capacity*
Lacks leadership skills	Has high leadership skills
Is inconsistent	Is consistent
Has anti-team philosophy	Supports team philosophy
Selects inappropriate members	Selects appropriate members
Lacks commitment to others on team	Is committed to others on team
Fails to build positive climate	Builds positive climate
Lacks concern to achieve	Is motivated by achievement
Is unclear about organizational role	Clearly defines organizational role

Lacks effective work methods	Uses effective work methods
Fails to define roles	Defines individual roles
Combines criticism and review	Reviews without personal criticism
Ignores individual development	Supports individual development
Subdues creative potential	Encourages creative potential
Tolerates poor intergroup relations	Develops sound intergroup relations
Allows conflict to be damaging	Uses conflict constructively

WHEN MANAGERS MOST NEED STRONG TEAMBUILDING CAPACITY

Teambuilding skills are relevant to all organizations that need to combine individual talents to achieve common goals. Their significance has increased dramatically in the second half of the twentieth century and is set to continue in the next as old organizational forms give way to more organic forms. Teams will increasingly become the building blocks of organizations. Many managers and supervisors spend more than 60 per cent of their time in meetings or otherwise operating in a group. Such members need a team approach to achieve their objectives, in particular managers of project groups, development teams, policy groups, service functions, and groups working under pressure.

Teambuilding skills are particularly important when a number of individuals must be brought together and learn to work cooperatively and effectively on common tasks. This frequently involves chairing meetings, representing groups and developing good relationships with other units in the organization. A manager consciously develops a team approach by sharing problems, developing a positive climate, clarifying goals and reviewing effectiveness regularly. These skills are most used when people are highly dependent on each other and need to work well together to achieve a good standard of output.

Other managers and supervisors work in relative isolation, perhaps contributing technical expertise, and they have less need for team development skills.

BLOCKAGE

11

INACTIVE PEOPLE DEVELOPMENT

It was an important day for John Truscott. At 31, he had achieved much in his career, and his energy and successes were legendary in his organization. His high level of achievement also applied to his personal life; he had an elegant house and a loving wife and was considered an excellent sailor, skier and golfer. In fact, John's neighbours thought that he lived like a Hollywood star and his colleagues believed he was earmarked for the higher reaches of the management world.

On this day, John was meeting the group managing director of his company to discuss his career and future. Naturally ambitious and confident, John expected to hear about the dramatic advances in store for him. At home he speculated with his wife, 'Perhaps it will be a business school, twelve weeks at Harvard, a period at the Geneva office, or even an assignment as personnel director to broaden my general management experience'. On his way to Group Headquarters, John felt a surge of excitement at the prospects and approached the managing director's door with eager anticipation.

He was greeted warmly and told, 'John, you are one of the finest of our younger managers. You have achieved much in your years with us and I want to compliment you on the energy, creativity and decisiveness that you show. I have been considering your future career and there is no doubt in my mind that you could hold a more senior position.' When the group managing director saw John almost visibly swell with pride, he decided to express his concern before the young man's expectations reached an impossibly high level. He frowned as he said, 'But John, I have to express a real problem that prevents me from promoting you now. You do not have a clear successor. The people in your department recognize your quality and are loyal to you, but none of them stands out. You have used them well, but you have not developed them. You are a star who shines too brightly alone. We need strength in the organization as a whole. That is a serious weakness and, until it is put right, there can be no promotion for you.'

John Truscott sat still, deflated and shocked. His thoughts raced through a series of defensive arguments, but the truth of the comments was impossible to deny. He responded with uncharacteristic simplicity, 'It's true, and I'll see that the matter is put right'.

DEVELOPMENT AS A KEY MANAGEMENT TASK

Every manager and supervisor must be concerned with developing all those they supervise. Sometimes development responsibilities extend wider – to colleagues, co-workers, network groups and, surprisingly, bosses. Managers need to be active in creating a learning organization.

We assume that most people have significant potential development; as the cost of human resources grows, it becomes more important to harness this potential. The development of people is a key aspect of managerial effectiveness, and it results in:

❏   More interest and excitement for the job holder
❏   Improved job performance
❏   Successors for senior posts
❏   Gains in vitality and a positive climate
❏   Continuous performance improvement.

Notice that several of these points refer to the effect of development on morale and vitality rather than straightforward performance criteria. This is important. For many people the enemy is within: rigidity and disillusionment rob them of their confidence and strength. Personal and professional development are powerful antidotes to emotional obsolescence. The manager who develops people is contributing to their energy resources as well as to their increased effectiveness.

People development brings organizational benefits. Since fundamental change, innovation and adaptation will be characteristics of many twenty-first century organizations, learning must be made a central theme – as important as quality, strategy and process effectiveness.

 ## THE MANAGER AS A TRAINER

This chapter examines the role of the manager or supervisor in developing subordinates. Many organizations have professional training staff who give advice, act as facilitators, conduct training courses, manage learning and assign people to management development programmes. However, this professional training role is a topic in itself and is not discussed here. We are concerned with what managers can do to develop their own skills as trainers and we examine the skills of:

1. Creating a climate for personal growth.
2. Assessing individual needs.
3. Counselling and coaching.
4. Learning from work experience.

In a sense, each manager and supervisor is a part-time trainer who is constantly developing people. Challenges of day-to-day work provide the raw material for learning. No one expects managers to possess the skills of professional trainers, but they do have one unique advantage in training: everything that happens at work is real. Genuine development must be reflected in day-to-day effectiveness.

 ## CREATING A CLIMATE FOR PERSONAL GROWTH

The group climate is substantially influenced, even created, by the attitudes and behaviour of managers. Workers watch carefully to see what their manager encourages and values or dismisses and punishes. It is how we behave, not what we say, that shapes climate.

The opinions of different managers concerning the development of others can vary a great deal. Expressed simply, any one of the following attitudes may be held:

❑   *Directive*:   instructing in detail.
❑   *Mechanistic*:   installing learning in systems and disciplines.
❑   *Negligent*:   ignoring the development of others.
❑   *Personal*:   helping individuals to learn from their own experience.
❑   *Protective*:   shielding people from the discomfort of risk.
❑   *Punishing*:   looking for errors or weaknesses and highlighting them.
❑   *Supportive*:   encouraging learning and experimentation.

There is a direct relationship between the attitudes of managers and the climates of their teams. One of the most striking effects of managerial attitude is seen in the amount of energy people are prepared to put into their own jobs and personal development. Some managers and supervisors create a climate that promotes energetic and constructive effort, while others affect their subordinates like a rainstorm during an open-air concert.

Individuals vary greatly in the commitment they put into their own development. Some devote themselves to increasing their capacities, while others allow their lives to drift by with the same involvement they would feel while watching a third-rate television play. For many people, the routines of daily living fail to stimulate more than a fraction of their available capacity, but in an emergency these same people can amaze themselves with extraordinary bursts of sustained and effective energy. An aim of development is to make extraordinary behaviour an everyday happening.

Effective managers and supervisors are deeply involved in helping to release and channel human energy. It is part of their role to unblock each individual's capacity and to find suitable vehicles for its expression. Some managers know how to create an excellent and stimulating environment, while others surround themselves with bored and sullen people whose personal development needs are unknown and unsatisfied.

DEVELOPING CRAFTSMANSHIP

Human capability can be thought of in terms of *craftsmanship*. A craftsman knows what raw materials are available and can fashion a high-quality product out of these resources. He is realistic and will only take achievable assignments. The word *craftsman* is usually applied to skilled manual workers, but the notion has more significance than this. The skills and approach of a craftsman are equally relevant to a factory cleaner and a research scientist. In every craft, from trapeze artist to piano tuner, ability has been acquired by studying the characteristics of high-quality performance and by painstakingly striving to gain the necessary knowledge and skills.

Craftsmen develop their competence in depth. They learn the skills of their trade but, more fundamentally, the underlying values and attitudes. Craftsmen love their work. They are fully committed to standards and learning. Their identity is firmly linked to their craft. As they become masters they train and develop others.

A manager or supervisor can apply the concept of craftsmanship by using the process illustrated in Figure 10. The manager asks 'What is the highest possible level of craftsmanship that could be achieved by this job holder?' When this question is answered specifically, the answer is compared with current performance, and the gap represents the development needed. Because genuine pride in work is only

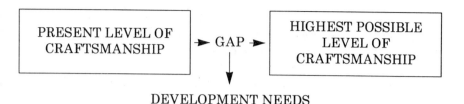

Figure 10 *Comparing present and possible levels of craftsmanship*

generated by above-average performance levels, it is a mistake to settle for an average performance.

The effective manager helps each subordinate to identify the gap between present performance and excellence and make tangible improvements in effectiveness. In the process, he/she aids each person's learning through appraisal of performance, coaching, counselling, feedback and using opportunities at work to increase experience.

 ## CHARACTERISTICS OF A LEARNING CLIMATE

If the group climate is one that encourages a real interest in learning, then many of the problems of human obsolescence are reduced. The concept of *obsolescence*, borrowed from mechanical design, has validity in relation to people. Individuals may be described as obsolescent when they are so hidebound in vision, adaptability and application that they cannot contribute to the development of their organization. Typically, an obsolescent person is well into middle age, but the roots of the condition are established in earlier years. This becomes apparent when we compare the different effects of ageing on people and observe that some have avoided the loss of energy and adaptability that usually comes with age.

By helping people to work for personal growth, managers and supervisors can develop a climate that reduces the effects of personal obsolescence. Obsolescence does not respect position and can be as insidious for the head of the company as for the electrician, so the manager also needs to take steps to remain open and flexible. A climate that supports personal learning will have many of the following characteristics:

❑ Excellence is frequently redefined and is a goal to be achieved.
❑ People objectively review their competence.
❑ Personal development is planned.

- ❏ Risks may be taken without fear of ridicule.
- ❏ Resources are allocated for personal development.
- ❏ Opportunities to develop people are seized whenever they are present.
- ❏ Coaching is common.
- ❏ All-round feedback is available.

 ## APPRAISAL

Managers and supervisors are asked to perform many difficult tasks and one of the most traumatic and sensitive is appraisal interviews in which the supervisor evaluates an employee's performance and presents the evaluation. This procedure encourages face-to-face feedback and discussion between the supervisor and the subordinate.

Many people dislike being evaluated, particularly if they are found wanting. It may well remind them of their school days. On the other hand, when asked to define their most valuable personal development experiences, some people recall their appraisal by an experienced person whose views they respected and valued.

Appraisals present both the boss and the subordinate with difficulties. The appraiser recognizes that it is hard to make objective evaluations and communicate them clearly and humanely. The person being appraised is likely to find the experience tense and perhaps embarrassing, as well as significant. It is not surprising, therefore, that appraisals are given too little time or are undertaken with inadequate preparation and skills. The appraisal process is at the heart of job-related training and the manager or supervisor can do much to aid individual learning through well-conducted appraisals.

Many organizations have instituted formal appraisal systems. Generally these require a manager to conduct annual appraisals with each subordinate. The key points of discussion are written down, and this document is kept in the confidential records of the company. It is a condition of most appraisal systems that an interview is held during which the individual is told about the assessment, and has the opportunity to ask questions and make comments.

CONDUCTING APPRAISAL INTERVIEWS

It is not uncommon for formal appraisals to go awry. The interview can be demoralizing or raise false expectations and the quality of information is often suspect and inadequate. Many subordinates feel that their appraisals have been too brief or badly handled and they fail to see the benefits of the process. It is one of the objectives of the system that the individuals appraised find the experience constructive and energizing. Another objective is that the organization obtains information necessary for planning its manpower strategies. For a formal appraisal to fulfil these objectives, certain steps should be taken. The following procedures are our suggestions for preparing an appraisal.

Step 1   Preparation

Before carrying out an appraisal find out about the particular system adopted by your company. This involves knowing the format for recording information but, more importantly, understanding how the information is going to be used. You will need to ensure that both you and the subordinate have the necessary paperwork to complete the project. Before an interview, determine whether you have the skills you need to handle the assignment effectively; a brief training programme can probably fill any gap. Asking for counsel from a colleague, in confidence, can help to clarify difficult issues.

Sometimes you can collect all-round feedback from subordinates, colleagues and bosses. This gives an excellent basis for appraisal. You need to set aside time for collecting the information on which the assessment will be made. At its best, a formal appraisal takes a long look backward over the past year and a full perspective on the year to come. To come to a balanced view, talk to those who receive a service from the person concerned, examine written or technical work and assess performance against goals that were previously set and recorded. Since the goal of all jobs is adding value to customers (internal or external), the views of customers must be sought. Several global companies now assess their executives on the basis of customer satisfaction surveys.

Step 2   Tuning for the Interview

Conduct appraisals in private, creating an atmosphere conducive to a frank, measured, and creative exchange. In these days of open-plan offices, you may have to book a suitable meeting place. Sufficient time should be set aside for the meeting; many managers say that two hours is reasonable.

As the appraiser, you need to prepare yourself psychologically and decide how you intend to approach the interview. Although you may be caught up in the immediate concerns of the day any such anxieties will prevent the balanced perspective needed for a successful interview. You need to 'tune' your mind so that you are relaxed and able to review performance over a reasonably long time-scale.

Step 3   The Interview

Before the interview, pay attention to the placing of the seats, layout of the room and noise level. Care must be taken to ensure that the subordinate is not placed at a psychological disadvantage. Likewise, it is inappropriate for the appraiser to sit on a chair several inches higher and peer down at the subordinate. Interruptions need to be prevented: don't allow a stream of telephone calls or messages during an interview.

First, check on whether you are feeling relaxed. Should you feel tense, ease the tension by talking about it and sharing your discomfort openly. The subordinate may also feel ill at ease and should be encouraged to talk about this. Anxieties are lessened when they are brought out into the open.

The objective of the interview must be clearly and positively stated and mutually accepted. Both the appraiser and the subordinate need to state what each wants to achieve. Each party could write down what he/she is seeking from the interview. When there is no agreement on basic objectives, little is achieved. If you are short of time, set priorities for the agenda and schedule a future time to complete the interview.

The interview is more likely to be successful when attitudes and feelings are openly expressed. It would be naive to expect that a managerial relationship characterized by a daily display of closed and sullen attitudes could suddenly bloom into an open and frank exchange of views on the one afternoon devoted to an appraisal. The best way to achieve openness is to set the tone for the interview by being open yourself.

Early in the interview, the agenda, or list of topics, should be worked through, agreed on and, perhaps, written down. It then becomes possible to evaluate the items and assign extra time to the more complex and important subjects. Each item on the agenda needs to be worked through in order to:

1. Define each area of the person's job and clarify aims and objectives.
2. Be very specific about criteria by which success may be judged.
3. Examine all the information that can assist the assessment of progress to date.
4. Identify any blockages to making progress and decide whether:
    (a) the subordinate should act differently;

(b)   you should act differently; or

(c)   some other resources are needed.

5.   Look ahead and clarify when progress can be usefully reviewed again.

This process may seem complicated and mechanistic but managers soon find ways to express the ideas in their own words. One manager described appraisal like this: 'Well, first you lay your cards on the table and agree on the contract – what you want and what he wants. Then you brainstorm topics to be worked through; list the items logically and problem-solve each one until it is resolved.' That is a description of appraisal in a nutshell. But often an appraisal becomes a stilted and clumsy discussion that both parties are happy to conclude as soon as decently possible.

Formal appraisals provide an opportunity to examine long-term career development and for this a spirit of realism is essential. Few can achieve high positions in an organization, but many aspire to them, so disappointment is inevitable. However, career development is possible for almost everyone, as long as it is distinguished from promotion and status. We define career development as 'making the most of the person's potential within the confines of the life situation'. This does not hold out the hope of unwarranted progress as it is quite false and unproductive to see career development as an escalator that only needs someone to stand on the bottom step and gradually be transported upward. People must realize that their progress depends on their performance and energy. They are owed no reward for being present; their usefulness is the sole criterion for advancement.

The appraiser's questions can do much to bring the subordinate's attitude and career goals out into the open. The result may be fantasy mixed with either undue hope or pessimism. The exposure of the subordinate's views and personal counselling of the kind described in the next few pages can bring realism and planning to this important aspect of working life. A systematic plan for personal development will often spring from a career review.

Step 4   Closing the Interview

Toward the end of the appraisal interview, review the meeting. This has three main purposes:

1.   Items are reconsidered and any outstanding matters are resolved.

2.   Any items that have not been satisfactorily discussed can be identified and a plan can be made to fill the gap.

3.   The extent to which joint objectives have been met can be evaluated.

One of the primary goals of the appraisal interview is to obtain information to help manage the staffing of the organization. Before the interview closes, check the extent to which this goal has been accomplished. Should there be any gaps, try to fill them. Most appraisal systems ask the subordinate to comment on the written report of the interview, so that any differences of view can be clearly identified and worked through.

As in any important business process, it helps to review the appraisal process and ask for feedback about its effectiveness. Both the manager and the subordinate need to express what they are feeling and thinking, and the subordinate's comments should be specifically elicited. If the experience has not been positive, then it should be examined to see whether anything can be done to improve it.

The appraisal process is an inherent part of the development process. If the methods and skills of appraisal are mastered, they provide a manager with a flexible and useful tool for improving relationships, developing individuals and helping an organization to coordinate human effort successfully.

Appraisal is not just a once-a-year event; manager and subordinate benefit when there is a contract for frequent two-way appraisal.

 ## COUNSELLING

Counselling can be defined as 'helping others work through problems and see opportunities more clearly'. It takes place informally every day. When conducted skilfully, counselling can have a significant impact on the way a person thinks and reacts. The skills of counselling assist the development of others and enlarge the manager's functions from a limited custodial role to a developmental role. Managers usually find that counselling is hard work and demands full attention.

COUNSELLING OPPORTUNITIES

Counselling begins with the intention to devote time, attention and skills to helping another person. Not only is the counselling process useful to any managers working with subordinates; it can also be used with colleagues, managers from other groups, and your own manager. Counselling is thus applicable whenever people confront difficult situations. The following list of counselling opportunities demonstrates some of the applications:

- ❑ Formal appraisal with subordinates
- ❑ Informal review meetings with subordinates
- ❑ Problem-solving discussions with other managers
- ❑ Career discussions and planning
- ❑ Conflict resolution
- ❑ Giving feedback at meetings
- ❑ Sorting out difficult relationships
- ❑ Helping friends in difficulties
- ❑ Asking for assistance for yourself.

DEVELOPING COUNSELLING SKILLS

Although counselling skills can be developed, they begin with an attitude. You can be helped by another person only if that person understands your dilemmas and you respect the other's contribution. Skilful counsellors adopt an open approach to life and work and try hard to follow these four principles:

1. They are genuine and mean what they say. They do not use counselling for manipulation or personal benefit.
2. They are concrete and clear so that their messages are understood directly.
3. They can see how the other person feels and accurately judge his or her state of mind.
4. They are prepared to uncover uncomfortable facts or feelings without losing basic respect for the other person.

Counselling is more than a set of skills; it is a two-way relationship that involves the participants fully. The aims of counselling are:

- ❑ To help the other person resolve problems and see opportunities.
- ❑ To help the other person become clearer about what is important.
- ❑ To help the other person express tensions and frustrations that may be obscuring important issues or facts.
- ❑ To help the other person take a more responsible attitude to his or her own life and be active in seeking rewarding achievements.

People with problems may feel that they are at a disadvantage and try to protect themselves from recognizing reality. For them, the exposure of a genuine problem seems to be an admission that they cannot cope, and this offends their image of strength and decisiveness.

A skilful counsellor will discern the problems that are expressed obliquely and the real issues that are hidden. Counselling requires skill and tenacity.

Counselling skills can be described briefly by arranging them on the scale shown in Figure 11. Shown at the top of the chart are skills used by a counsellor to encourage the other person to structure his or

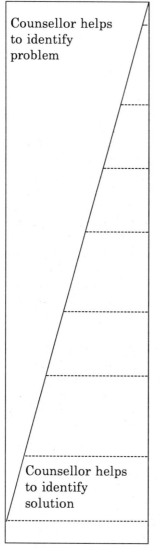

Counsellor helps to identify problem

Listening: encouraging the person to speak and clarify his/her views through expression

Clarifying: checking that you understand what the person is saying and meaning

Summarizing: pulling together threads so that the whole picture can be seen

Probing: asking specific questions to clarify your understanding and allow the person to explore his/her views further

Defining: trying to define and label the issue problem or opportunity

Reviewing options: evaluating different ways the issue, problem or opportunity can be progressed

Recommending: coming to a conclusion and suggesting the best way to act

Counsellor helps to identify solution

Prescribing: telling the other person what to do

Figure 11 A scale of counselling skills

her own thoughts and solve the problem from within. The skills in the lower part of the scale are used as the counsellor moves toward solving the problem on behalf of the other person.

There is an appropriate time to use each of the eight techniques shown on the scale. It is a common error for counsellors to use the techniques listed at the bottom of the scale and make recommendations prematurely. Most counsellors find that they have to work hard at becoming more skilful at the techniques listed at the top of the scale – helping others to solve their own problems.

The two people in a counselling relationship should begin a session, however informal, by agreeing on what outcomes they want from the session. This helps to start the session moving and allows the counsellor to identify the role he/she can most usefully play. By all means discuss whether to use an approach that focuses on problems or on solutions, as explained in Figure 11.

When people identify some of the most significant experiences in their personal development, they talk about particular people who have given them direct and pertinent information about themselves. This was feedback, and it has so much impact that it can profoundly influence the way in which people operate. Feedback, like many powerful tools, can be abused. People have been hurt or deflated through receiving feedback, so managers need to find ways of giving feedback so that others become stronger and more effective.

Many people have to work for some time to develop the skills of giving feedback effectively. Once acquired, this capacity is an extremely valuable management asset and it can influence and improve many aspects of personal life. The following guidelines indicate how effective feedback can be given as part of the counselling process.

Give your full attention

> Because you will be giving information that is deeply personal, give your full attention to the encounter. Ensure that distractions are eliminated and devote yourself fully to the other person.

Be sensitive to the other person

> Before you start, determine whether your own intentions are clear and positive. Sometimes counsellors have harmful emotional objectives which, if expressed, can result in a sour and unhelpful encounter.

Check to see whether your feedback is welcome

> Your opinions and reactions will be most useful when the other person has invited your comments. This increases receptivity and provides a basis for openness. It also encourages the other person to help you discuss the most relevant areas.

Express yourself directly

> Good feedback is clear and specific. Timidity and vague comments are enemies of direct and useful feedback.

Express your views fully

If feedback is not explored in enough depth, the receiver has only a superficial understanding of your meaning. This provides insufficient basis for change. Expressing your thoughts and feelings as fully as possible allows the recipients of feedback to evaluate the impact of their behaviour.

Separate fact from opinion

You should be able to provide objective information about a person's behaviour and express your reaction to it. Both are relevant but be careful to distinguish between fact and opinion. Usually the most helpful feedback concentrates on information rather than opinion and avoids judgement or evaluation. Simply describing the situation as you see it allows the other person to make the evaluation. If the giver of feedback wants to express judgements, he/she must state clearly that these are matters of subjective evaluation.

Think about timing

The most useful feedback is given when the recipient is receptive and sufficiently close to the event being discussed for it to be fresh in his/her mind. Storing comments can lead to recriminations and reduce effectiveness. The principle is to give feedback regularly and give it immediately.

Give practical help

Useful feedback leads to a change in behaviour. Hence the most useful feedback is concerned with behaviour that the recipient can change. Giving feedback about matters outside a person's control is less directly useful. Suggesting alternative ways of behaving can help the person think through new ways of tackling problems.

Ensure that your message is heard

When possible, check with other people to see if they agree with you. This is especially useful in a training group and can also be promoted in a work team. When different viewpoints are collected and assimilated, points of difference and similarity can be clarified and a more objective picture developed.

USES OF FEEDBACK

It is difficult for some people to express positive feelings. They feel embarrassed or simply do not know how to give approval or warmth to others. The person who leaves such feedback unexpressed deprives others of much that could help them enjoy life and develop personal strength. There are serious drawbacks to the withholding of either negative or positive feedback because both organizations and individuals thrive on open expression. From many points of view, acquiring skill in giving and receiving feedback greatly increases an individual's value as a manager, a professional worker and a friend.

 LEARNING FROM WORK EXPERIENCE

COACHING

Many day-to-day challenges offer opportunities for personal development. Coaching is a training technique that uses the real world; the most valid source of development is often tackling genuine problems. The essence of coaching is the immediate interaction between action and learning. The coach manages a learning cycle as shown in Figure 12. The aims of coaching are:

❑ To develop the potential of subordinates.
❑ To energize and motivate others, using the realism and vitality that inevitably come with the real world.
❑ To ease the manager's work load and develop skills of delegation.

There are two forms of coaching. First, the daily ebb and flow of work creates many opportunities. Just as a sports coach works to improve the skills of athletes, so the manager can find a myriad of ways to make encounters become learning opportunities.

Second, coaching is used to structure assignments outside the current job scope, extending both experience and competence. One of

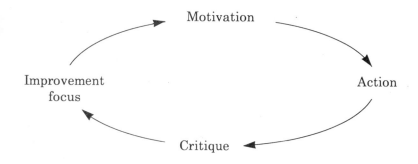

Figure 12 The learning cycle

the most difficult aspects of coaching is choosing assignments that extend people without overstretching them. This second level of coaching grows into action learning. The principle is clear. People gain from achievement of new and stretching tasks in the messy real world. It is the role of the coach to intervene at appropriate points. The assignments should be real tasks that have a practical purpose, such as:

❑   Attending more senior meetings
❑   Undertaking projects
❑   Meeting customers
❑   Consulting with other departments
❑   Making decisions in new areas of responsibility
❑   Analysing information.

PHASES IN JOB PROGRESSION

Coaching is not just constructive for those who are new to a job; it can be just as relevant for long-established employees. As a person becomes familiar with a new job, whether menial or managerial, a predictable pattern of changes usually takes place. The main phases of this change pattern are shown in Figure 13 and can be described as follows:

Phase One: Challenge

A new job makes many demands. Credibility must be established, new facts assimilated, and appropriate decisions taken. Assignments may be lengthy because the new person has not found the optimum way of tackling them. This is a time that stretches and challenges the individual who is trying to get 'on top' of the job.

Phase two: Competence

As individuals learn and develop, they begin to set their own standards for performance and to meet them. Relationships continue to be built as support from colleagues grows. Each new demand or item of information is no longer a cause of uncertainty. Usually the speed and certainty of response is greatly improved.

Phase Three: Mastery

After a considerable period in the job, the challenges become less and the individual finds that most demands can be met readily from

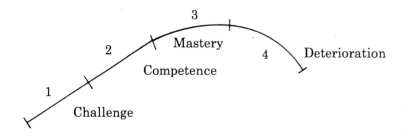

Figure 13 Four stages of progression in a job

accumulated experience. Systems, both formal and informal, cope with large amounts of routine business and a wider perspective is possible. The person may undertake special projects to explore the wider possibilities of the job but essentially there is still interest and room to expand in it.

Phase Four: Deterioration

This phase is not inevitable but often occurs as the stimulation of the job becomes weaker and the person fails to seek out new challenges. Some people lapse into conventional routines and grow so habit-bound that their capacity to adapt withers. Others seek outlets for their initiative and creativity outside the organization.

COACHING SKILLS

The skills required for coaching are basic to any effective manager:

☐   To interact in the learning process
☐   To observe
☐   To support the learner
☐   To help the learner analyse shortcomings and strengths
☐   To set clear and attainable goals/objectives
☐   To be aware of the feelings and needs of others.

The coaching approach offers several distinctive benefits:
1.   It leads to real development.
2.   Useful work is undertaken alongside development.
3.   It improves the relationship between manager and subordinate.

4. Costs are low.

5. It is directly related to the specific needs of the person.

However, there are also pitfalls that can limit the effectiveness of the approach. The success of coaching depends on the competence of the coach. Time needs to be spent on finding assignments, counselling and monitoring.

 ## THE LEARNING ORGANIZATION

The personal skills that we have described in this chapter are part of a broader theme. In recent years we have come to realize that knowledge in itself is a source of competitive advantage. This point is made clear by an example. Ask 'What distinguishes the Harvard Business School from your local University?' and you will see that the accumulated expertise residing in Harvard is its most significant strength. Of course, the knowledge is dispersed, in computers, books, systems, people's heads, work processes, or in the culture and processes of the organization. But this knowledge, combined with the capacity to apply it consistently, is an incomparable resource.

Knowledge increases daily and some unlearning must take place. It is just as important to shed obsolete practices and attitudes as to acquire new ones. Given the importance of acquiring organizational knowledge, the process cannot be left to chance. Managers can take the following steps:

1. Review the processes for learning that currently operate in their area of responsibility.
2. Look at similar organizations which are recognized as excellent examples of type and compare.
3. Assess what customers want now and in the future.
4. Collect ideas from all your staff as to what learning they want and need.
5. Identify the blockages to excellent performance in the group or organization.
6. Establish learning goals for each individual and group.
7. Develop a culture of learn-as-you-go.
8. Use the best resources for learning and development.
9. Apply the principles of action learning described earlier.

As learning becomes part of the organization's culture, people's resistance breaks down and they adopt a willingness to be open to seeing things differently. There is a refreshing humility when even the chairman of the board takes time for self-development and, more importantly, ceases to try to present an image to the world of complete competence. This attitude is well exemplified by Bill Gates, founder of Microsoft, which became one of the world's most powerful corporations in the 1990s. Gates prizes learning and puts it high on his agenda. He studies widely and deeply and is moved by what he learns. Whether Microsoft remains a top performer rests in part on the company's capacity to learn 'faster than the other guys'. This mission is so profound that it engages every member of the company in managing the learning process.

 ## CHARACTERISTICS OF MANAGERS WHO ARE ACTIVE/INACTIVE PEOPLE DEVELOPERS

Managers and supervisors who are responsible for others need to constantly improve their competence in people development. The characteristics of those who are active in this area are listed on the right-hand side of the following summary. The characteristics of those who are not active are listed on the left.

Inactive development	Active development
Ignores training aspect of job	Functions as a part-time trainer
Fails to create a positive climate for learning	Creates a positive climate for learning
Is unaware of learning needs of others	Helps analyse learning needs of others
Does not set challenging assignments	Establishes challenges for others
Uses appraisal casually	Systematically appraises people
Does not clarify strengths and weaknesses of subordinates	Clarifies strengths and weaknesses of subordinates
Ignores potential of others	Respects potential of others
Does not set stretching goals	Sets stretching goals
Underestimates importance of career development	Helps others plan their career development
Allows obsolescence to occur	Takes steps to avoid obsolescence
Is unskilled at giving feedback	Gives feedback skilfully
Counsels casually	Counsels others methodically
Fails to utilise development opportunities at work	Uses work opportunities for development

Weak coach	Strong coach
Not part of the 'learning organization'	Part of the 'learning organization'

WHEN MANAGERS MOST NEED TO DEVELOP OTHERS

All managers and supervisors who have day-to-day contact with other people need to acquire training skills. People development is most important where knowledge is needed for competitive advantage, where job demands are changing, and where departments comprise people who stay in the same job for a long time. In this last case, training and development are needed for motivation. Training skills are useful to those whose jobs require a high ability to influence others. There is a narrow distinction between influence and training, and those in such jobs frequently find that they need to encourage learning by others in order to achieve their own objectives.

BLOCKAGE

12

WEAK CUSTOMER FOCUS

It was a glum meeting. A few weeks before everything had looked promising. The company was working towards delivery of its biggest export order ever. The new night shift was working with a will; employees were excited; and the trades unions were positive. A huge critical path plan ran down the wall in the project manager's office.

The export manager opened the meeting by saying, 'I think we've blown it. All these last-minute problems have sunk us. I can't believe we will now meet the shipment dates. The question is why? What has gone wrong? We've planned this one to the smallest degree and it has still failed?

Discussion followed with everyone defending their own group's performance. Blame passed from hand to hand like a rugby ball. No one accepted responsibility. After fifteen minutes the project manager called the meeting to order and gazed disconsolately into his coffee cup. He said, 'It's now clear to me what went wrong. Everyone accepted responsibility for their part of the process but no one thought about the linkage between groups or about managing the process as a whole. We've failed because we have managed teams as separate units but not as interfacing ones. That's been our failure of management.'

This assessment was agreed but the managers were still unsure about how to proceed. They understood what needed to be done but not how to do it. At this point one of the more junior managers produced a management magazine from his briefcase and asked tentatively, 'I wonder whether this would help? Apparently many firms are moving to the idea that each department needs to see itself as a service provider to other groups and to negotiate service contracts with explicit deliverables – apparently that's one way of managing linkages.'

The idea was a new one to the group but, partly in desperation, they decided to try the procedures suggested in the article. By the end of the meeting 'service contracts' were established between groups. Then came a stroke of luck – the local airport in the customer's country was closed by industrial action and the extra three days were sufficient to complete the work and get the order delivered 'as soon as practical'.

All organizations can have difficulty in being customer-focused. Doctors in hospitals think they know more about the patients' experience than the patients themselves, shops make assumptions about what shoppers value and manufacturers design products which don't meet customers' requirements. Anyone who has tried to assemble a toy on Christmas Day (connect part B7 to the unit Z18 with grommet A4 using link A63) knows just how easy it is for a firm to lose customer focus.

Creating, informing, understanding and responding to customers is a key dimension of management. We have learned that everyone benefits from seeing others as customers – particularly within organizations. It looks simple but the concept is profound: individuals and groups are consumers of goods and services and need to be treated as honoured customers.

The point becomes clearer as we examine the example of the finance function in a medium-sized firm. Who are its customers? In no particular order the following list can be compiled:

❑   Customer 1 – The auditor, who needs legally acceptable accounts.
❑   Customer 2 – The tax man, in case he calls.
❑   Customer 3 – Shareholders, who need to know what profit they are making.
❑   Customer 4 – The managing director, who needs to understand profit, loss and costs.
❑   Customer 5 – Senior managers, who want to run business areas effectively.
❑   Customer 6 – Middle managers, who need information on costs, performance, etc.
❑   Customer 7 – Trades union representatives, who need to assess the company's wealth.

We shall not continue. It is sufficient to note that there are at least seven customer groups each with distinct wants and needs. The finance function must understand each client group's requirements and structure itself to provide as many as is reasonable.

WHAT IS A CUSTOMER?

Customers are direct or indirect users of goods or services produced by an individual, team, department or organization. In the simplest case a production line operator sits in a chair and receives half-assembled products on a moving belt. He/she adds several components and places the unit on the belt to be carried to the next operator. The next operator is the direct customer but there may be several levels of indirect customer, as shown in Figure 14.

Clearly each person or team is both a receiver of goods and/or services and a supplier of goods and/or services. Take the example of a teacher in a classroom. A 'map' showing supplier/customer relationships might look as in Figure 15.

Figure 15 is interesting because it questions conventional principles of organization. For example the head teacher is seen as a supplier rather than as a controller. Conceptualizing the firm as a network of supplier/customer relationships offers a powerful insight into the nature of cooperation in organizations.

MAPPING CUSTOMERS

Since customers are stakeholders in the output of the individual or organization it follows that we need to understand the requirements of all customers to illuminate their different wants and needs – which may be so diverse as to be contradictory. This is done by a process of 'mapping'. Each employee, team and organization needs to:
1.   List all their customers (both direct and indirect).

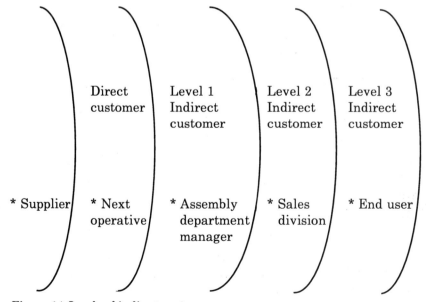

Figure 14 Levels of indirect customer

SUPPLIERS   CUSTOMERS

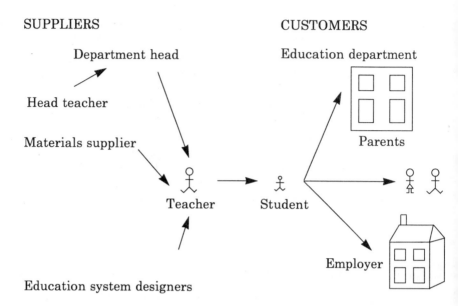

Figure 15 Map of supplier/customer relationships in the classroom

2. Find out what these customers want and need.
3. Define the gap between what is currently offered and what is desired.
4. Decide what is reasonable to offer (not all wants and needs can be fulfilled).
5. Specify a 'service contract' which specifies deliverables.
6. Set up a measuring and monitoring system.

Customer mapping is time-consuming since it is impossible to define a customer's wants and needs without analysis, discussion and debate. Also the exercise is rarely completed: wants and needs change and so service contracts need to be renegotiated to reflect the new requirements.

 PROCESS MANAGEMENT

As customers and suppliers are identified it often becomes apparent that there are linkages between groups, departments and organizational units. Often these linkages function poorly. This is because, historically, management attention has been focused on teams and departments rather than processes which stretch across organizations. Information and managerial technologies now permit much greater control over organizational processes, thereby allowing structures to be realigned to be more process- and customer-oriented.

No manager can be effective without developing good processes. In a sense an organization is like an orchestra: the string section may be playing sweetly but with a different tune from the woodwind – the result is a discordant cacophony. All parts of the organization need to play the same tune. Process management requires:

❑ Mapping existing processes both within and between departments
❑ Simplifying processes to remove unnecessary or wasteful elements
❑ Deciding who manages processes and sub-processes
❑ Determining and installing measures of process effectiveness
❑ Realigning responsibilities so the new organization works efficiently and effectively
❑ Learning from both successes and failures.

Interestingly, managers can use these techniques in their own areas of responsibility. Take a real, if simple, example. In a family the post arrives each morning and is sometimes placed on the hall table, sometimes in the kitchen. When a bill arrives sometimes it is separated from the rest of the post; sometimes the husband pays it; sometimes the wife pays it. Perhaps the husband pays for items that his wife has returned to the shop. Perhaps the bill is discarded with the opened envelopes. The cheque stub may be filled in or left blank. And so it goes on. Wasted effort, confusion and uncertainty characterize the process. If the husband and wife sit down and analyse what they *should* do the resulting process map might look as in Figure 16.

Clarifying the elements in a process brings any shortcomings in the existing system into sharp relief. Once recognized it is relatively easy to find solutions to problems and implement techniques of continuous improvement.

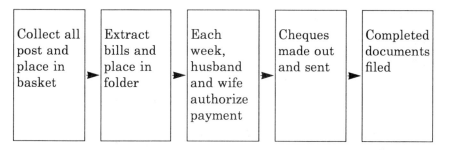

Figure 16 Process map for the family post

To bring about process improvements the following are needed:

- ❑ A climate of cooperation and mutual support
- ❑ Rewards for working with others
- ❑ Skills in bringing issues to the surface
- ❑ Techniques for differentiating between cause and effect
- ❑ Capacity to generate alternative and creative solutions
- ❑ Willingness to negotiate and form collaborative arrangements.

CONTRACTING

Improving processes may appear to be a technical task. In fact, the opposite is the case. Managing linkages between departments is an intensely human endeavour as it depends on people getting together and sorting out boundary disputes with a 'win–win' attitude.

Relationships between customers, suppliers and those who contribute to linked processes are codified and formalized using the powerful and flexible concept of 'contracting'.

A contract is a negotiated agreement in which each side has specific expectations of how the other will perform. Take another simple example. A child asks her mother, 'Can I go out to play?' Mother says, 'Certainly, but I want you to stay in the garden and not get wet'. 'Right,' says the child. 'What are you going to do?' asks the mother, to check that all her instructions are understood. 'I'm allowed to play but I mustn't go out of the garden and I must not get wet,' says the child. The mother and daughter now have a 'contract' – each has explicit expectations of the other and an agreement has been reached.

Of course, at this level 'contracting' takes place all the time but in organizational life it is far more common to witness contracts between bosses and subordinates than between customers and suppliers. Indeed, in bureaucratic organizations the customer/supplier linkages are managed by formalized systems and procedures. However, bureaucratic formalization is ill-suited to managing in a challenging and changing environment and the more flexible techniques of contracting become appropriate.

Take a personnel manager servicing a major department in a chemical company. Each year the personnel manager conducts an extended interview with the senior line manager and asks these questions:

❑   What 'deliverables' do you want from personnel in the next year?
❑   For each 'deliverable' what would define success?
❑   What would you find unacceptable? Be specific.
❑   What are our current strengths that you wish to see maintained?
❑   What are our current weaknesses that you wish to see improved?
❑   How much are you prepared to pay for each element in the service?
❑   What access and resources are you prepared to offer?
❑   How will we measure the performance of personnel?

As these questions are debated the expectations of the line manager become clearer. Naturally wants and needs may be suggested which either cannot be delivered or will require additional resources. These must be identified at this stage.

The personnel manager will take away the notes from the interview and develop a 'service agreement'. Those elements which are contentious must be highlighted for further debate. The aim is to produce a written agreement which both parties can use as a template for assessing what the personnel service ought to be. Since measures are built into the system any deviation from standards quickly becomes visible.

Annual contracting processes are adequate in many organizations but there is an implicit assumption of relative stability. In more turbulent times it may be impossible or undesirable to try to contract for a year – in which case it is more sensible to have frequent updates, but the contracting process remains the same.

Contracting is a powerful tool, indispensable in managing many interface relationships where there is no one line of authority. The skills of contracting should be part of every manager's tool-kit. They include:

❑   Active listening
❑   Questioning
❑   Summarizing
❑   Checking understanding
❑   Developing hypotheses
❑   Proposing
❑   Recording
❑   Negotiating
❑   Establishing measures
❑   Working to agreed disciplines.

THE END USER CUSTOMER

Imagine a factory worker sitting on a metal stool peering into what looks like a fish tank. The operator uses two remote arms to pick up tiny pellets of chemicals to insert into an industrial lamp. Each lamp takes about 30 seconds to complete, that is about 850 per day, or 205,000 per year.

This factory worker is producing a lamp which costs about US$20 and once fitted (probably in a street lamp) it will be expensive to replace. The end user customer wants quality, reliability and the lowest price possible. The question is, 'How can the factory assembly worker feel directly associated with the end user customer?'

The management task is to communicate meaning so that each completed lamp is felt to have value rather than be the focus of anger and alienation. This can be done directly by linking the operator with the customer and indirectly by creating an environment in which people feel wanted, valued and recognized.

One of the first organizations to recognize the link between managing meaning and customer service was the British retailer Marks and Spencer. Working in a shop can be a tiring, stressful and mundane experience. Streams of customers continuously spoil the symmetry of well-arranged clothing or other products on display. For each customer a purchase is significant; for the sales assistant it is one incident in thousands. Marks and Spencer's management realized more than 50 years ago that they could not engineer a situation in which each customer was treated as a respected individual unless they created a 'feel-good' response by employees toward the firm. A myriad of initiatives, from subsidized hairdressing to foot-care clinics, help create a positive response towards the company. Once this 'goodwill' is present it can be directed towards customer service. As there is no residue of anger or disappointment towards the employer, the customer is likely to be treated well. It works so satisfactorily that few shoppers find cause to complain about what they call 'the attitude' of M & S sales staff.

MOMENTS OF TRUTH

One of the authors was travelling from Hong Kong to Dubai with children. The flight attendant came along with a Polaroid camera and snapped the children playing with their bags of toys and games: a visit to the flight deck quickly followed. By the time they reached Dubai it was easy to see how Emirates had won the airline of the year award that year. However, as we shall see, a competitive edge this year becomes commonplace next year.

Emirates[1] had recognized that when a passenger interacts with staff on an airline flight those brief encounters are 'moments of truth' – brief exchanges which determine the passenger's emotional reaction to the company. Moments of truth are particularly important when something goes wrong or emotions are highly charged. Judgement and feelings are determined by a small number of highly significant 'moments of truth'.

The concept is so fundamental that it can provide unexpected advantages. Research evidence shows that if something goes wrong but the firm recovers well, the customer's loyalty is increased, not diminished, even though he or she was disadvantaged by the error. A personal experience makes the point. Dave Francis was flying from Hong Kong to London on Virgin Atlantic. His seat sound system failed and he was eventually moved to another seat. Next day, however, there was a phone call of apology, 20,000 additional air miles and a £25 voucher to soothe ruffled feelings. The result? Dave's preferred airline to Hong Kong is now Virgin Atlantic. His experience was obviously not unique for as we write Virgin has just been voted 'Airline of the Year', 'Best Transatlantic Carrier', 'Best Business/Executive Class', 'Best Ground Crew and Check-in Staff', 'Best In-flight Food and Wine' and 'Best In-flight Magazine'.

Managers can take these steps to use the moments-of-truth concept with both their direct and indirect customers:

❑   List your customers
❑   Interview to find out what is really important to them
❑   Identify those things that if done badly will create a 'feel-bad' reaction
❑   Identify those things that if done well will delight the customer
❑   Establish what behaviours are needed from your staff
❑   Use supervision, communication, systems and training to reinforce the desired behaviours
❑   Monitor how well you are performing on moments of truth
❑   Compare how well your competitors are performing on the same criteria.

---

[1] This approach was pioneered by Scandinavian Airlines (SAS).

CUSTOMER ORIENTATION

We shall continue to take our example from the airline industry. In the 1980s British Airways was a vast airline system with a poor reputation, noted for barely adequate customer service. By the 1990s it had been transformed, sometimes winning prizes as the airline offering the best travel experience. This reversal of fortunes (matched by a much improved financial performance) was partly helped by what may appear to have been a bizarre management decision: much of the engineering function was structured to report to the main board through the marketing division. The rationale was simple but profound. Hitherto engineers thought that only engineering criteria were important in decision making. Once marketing had an influence this idea changed so that engineering decisions were taken in the context of the customer-oriented marketing mission of British Airways.

No management initiative gives strength for ever, and British Airways will need to be innovative in meeting customer aspirations or it will decline in ratings, popularity and profitability.

Every manager can take steps to be more customer-oriented. Hospitals must see patients as customers, tax offices should see the public as their customers and TV companies should adopt a similar approach to their viewers. This approach greatly assists the organization to be genuinely customer-led – essential in all winning organizations. Characteristics of managers with weak customer focus are listed on the left; characteristics of managers with strong customer focus are listed on the right.

Weak customer focus	*Strong customer focus*
Is not concerned for customers	Is concerned for customers
Does not set success criteria in terms of customer satisfaction	Sets success criteria in terms of customer satisfaction
Sees other departments as adversaries	Sees other departments as colleagues
Fails to see an organization as a chain of customers and suppliers	Sees an organization as a chain of customers and suppliers
Maintains low communication with internal/external customers	Maintains high communication with internal/external customers
Does not analyse customer relationships	Analyses customer relationships

Does not enter into contracts with customers	Enters into contracts with customers
Does not seek to delight customers in moments of truth	Seeks to delight customers in moments of truth

 ## WHEN MANAGERS MOST NEED CUSTOMER FOCUS

The concept of customer focus is becoming more important as the world increasingly becomes a 'global village'. As external customers are chased by more and more competing organizations managers in organizations characterized by internal strife and disagreement or by low external customer satisfaction need to address the issue of customer focus with urgency.

ASSESSING MANAGERIAL
CAPABILITY

THE BLOCKAGE SURVEY (OTHER)

Everyone benefits from feedback on how they perform their job. To do this, we invite you to invite others to complete the Blockage Survey (Other) about you. This will help you to gain another perspective on your strengths and personal blockages.

USING THE BLOCKAGE SURVEY (OTHER)

PURPOSE

To provide a framework for collecting data on personal strengths and blockages.

TIME

Approximately twenty minutes to complete the survey.

MATERIALS

The survey is set out on the next few pages, but the answer sheet may be photocopied if you do not want to mark your book.[1]

---

[1] This instrument is the copyright of Challenge Ltd, from whom additional copies may be obtained. Contact Challenge Ltd, Challenge House, 45/47 Victoria Street, Mansfield, Notts. NG18 5SU. Tel.: 01623 645901. Fax: 01623 22621.

METHOD

1.   Select people who can give you feedback on your management capability. We suggest your boss, some colleagues and your own direct staff.
2.   Speak to the respondents and tell them about your aims and procedures for completion.
3.   When your respondents have completed the survey, consider the results carefully to assess how valid they are for you.

A NOTE OF CAUTION

Although the survey is methodical and logical, it reflects one person's subjective views and it should therefore be seen as an aid to self-review rather than as a scientific measure.

Name of person being reviewed ....

 THE BLOCKAGE SURVEY (OTHER)

INSTRUCTIONS FOR COMPLETING THE SURVEY

By completing this questionnaire you can give valuable feedback to the manager whose name is at the top of this page.

On the following pages, you will find five sections. You need to complete each section in the same way.

For each section you have 20 points which *must* be allocated. Look over the list of items and allocate the points to represent the reviewee's personal development needs as you see them.

One item can receive all twenty points, or you can spread the points over as many items as you wish – the aim is to highlight the reviewee's development needs.

SECTION ONE

Allocate 20 points between these twelve items.

This manager would be more effective if he/she did the following things more or better . . .

1. maintained a high level of personal energy ☐
2. knew where he/she stood on matters of principle ☐
3. had a clear 'vision' of what needs to be done ☐
4. provided creative ideas ☐
5. took his/her own development seriously ☐
6. solved problems in a structured way ☐
7. set clear goals for others ☐
8. motivated those who work for him/her ☐
9. managed projects effectively ☐
10. built high-performing teams ☐
11. created opportunities to help others to develop ☐
12. focused on satisfying customers (internal or external) ☐

SECTION TWO

Allocate 20 points between these twelve items.

This manager could improve these activities . . .

13. seeking outside assessments of his/her group's efficiency

14. holding regular coaching sessions with his/her staff

15. leading teams towards achieving shared objectives

16. making better use of available resources

17. taking a firm line with low-performing people

18. running productive meetings

19. developing a wider range of options before taking a decision

20. setting time aside for his/her own learning

21. suggesting radical ways to improve processes

22. obtaining other people's commitment to his/her objectives

23. dealing confidently with decisions that involve finely-balanced value judgements

24. managing his/her own time efficiently

SECTION THREE

Allocate 20 points between these twelve items.

This manager would perform better if he/she . . .

25. reduced his/her personal stress level

26. operated from a coherent 'philosophy' of management

27. enrolled others to support his/her initiatives

28. suggested more innovative ideas

29. set demanding development objectives for him/herself

30. took more time for decision making when issues are important

31. measured other people's performance objectively

32. gave greater emotional support to others

33. delegated effectively

34. developed a more positive climate in teams

35. gave counselling to his/her staff

36. worked co-operatively with other departments
     and teams

SECTION FOUR

Allocate 20 points between these twelve items.

This manager would be more skilful if he/she . . .

37. sought regular feedback about performance from
     internal or external customers

38. actively provided opportunities for staff to develop
     their abilities

39. helped work groups to clarify their team development
     needs

40. designed effective work processes

41. communicated systematically to his/her staff

42. ensured that key objectives are measured

43. consciously involved others in decision making

44. tried new ideas to extend his/her own experience

45. seized opportunities that others miss

46. enrolled others in his/her vision of what needs to be
     done

47. fundamentally questioned his/her own values from time
     to time

48. dealt with setbacks without losing confidence

SECTION FIVE

Allocate 20 points between these twelve items.

To develop further this manager needs to . . .

49. maintain a higher level of energy

50. behave in ways that are consistent with his/her beliefs ☐

51. be more assertive ☐

52. maintain effort when solutions cannot be readily found ☐

53. learn from honest feedback on his/her own strengths and weaknesses ☐

54. handle complex information with clarity and confidence ☐

55. monitor progress towards the achievement of goals ☐

56. supervise others flexibly according to each person's individual needs ☐

57. organize people and resources efficiently ☐

58. develop high-performing teams ☐

59. comprehensively appraise the performance of subordinates ☐

60. developing a clear understanding of his/her customers' (internal or external) needs ☐

ANSWER GRID FOR THE BLOCKAGE SURVEY (OTHER)

Copy the numbers for each of the five sections onto the answer grid below and add the scores for each horizontal line.

Totals

1	24	25	48	49		
						1
2	23	26	47	50		
						2
3	22	27	46	51		
						3
4	21	28	45	52		
						4
5	20	29	44	53		
						5
6	19	30	43	54		
						6
7	18	31	42	55		
						7
8	17	32	41	56		
						8
9	16	33	40	57		
						9
10	15	34	39	58		
						10
11	14	35	38	59		
						11
12	13	36	37	60		
						12

Now transfer the numbers to the next page.

SCORING SHEET FOR THE BLOCKAGE SURVEY (OTHER)

INSTRUCTIONS

1. Enter the total from the answer grid sheet for each of the 12 categories in the *Your score* column.
2. Fill in the *Ranking* column by giving your highest score a ranking of 1, the second highest score a ranking of 2 and continue. The lowest score is ranked 12.

	YOUR SCORE	RANKING	BLOCKAGE
1			Incompetent self-management
2			Negative personal values
3			Inferior leadership vision
4			Low creativity
5			Passive personal development
6			Unstructured problem solving and decision making
7			Unclear goals
8			Negative management style
9			Poor organizing skills
10			Weak team-building capacity
11			Inactive people development
12			Weak customer focus

WHAT DO THE SCORES MEAN?

The highest scores represent another person's viewpoint of the possible blockages to you achieving your management potential. Use this data to help you decide which blockages you want to explore further.

INDEX

communication of   163
defined   130
see also Managerial vision

Wages *see* Remuneration
Weight (monitoring of)   37
Winning (from a values perspective)
  56

Work environment (motivation
  considerations)   32, 149, 158
Workload   43, 48
Workload reorganization (in
  teambuilding)   181
Writing (as an aid to self–insight)
  100